OPPOSING VIEWPOINTS® SERIES

Sexually Transmitted Diseases

W9-DCF-040

Other Books of Related Interest:

Opposing Viewpoints Series
Africa

AIDS

Education

Sex

Teenage Sexuality

Current Controversies Series
Gay Rights

Homosexuality

Sexually Transmitted Diseases

At Issue Series
AIDS in Developing Countries

How Does Religion Influence Politics?

Sex Education

Sexually Trasmitted Diseases

The Spread of AIDS

Teen Sex

"Congress shall make
no law . . . abridging
the freedom of speech,
or of the press."

First Amendment to the U.S. Constitution

The basic foundation of our democracy is the First Amendment guarantee of freedom of expression. The Opposing Viewpoints Series is dedicated to the concept of this basic freedom and the idea that it is more important to practice it than to enshrine it.

**OPPOSING
VIEWPOINTS®
SERIES**

Sexually Transmitted Diseases

Margaret Haerens, Book Editor

GREENHAVEN PRESS

An imprint of Thomson Gale, a part of The Thomson Corporation

THOMSON

™

GALE

Detroit • New York • San Francisco • New Haven, Conn. • Waterville, Maine • London

Christine Nasso, *Publisher*
Elizabeth Des Chenes, *Managing Editor*

© 2006 Thomson Gale, a part of The Thomson Corporation.

Thomson and Star logo are trademarks and Gale and Greenhaven Press are registered trademarks used herein under license.

For more information, contact: Greenhaven Press
27500 Drake Rd.
Farmington Hills, MI 48331-3535
Or you can visit our Internet site at http://www.gale.com

Cover photograph reproduced by permission of Photos.com.

LIBRARY OF CONGRESS CATALOGING-IN-PUBLICATION DATA

Sexually transmitted diseases / Margaret Haerens, book editor.
    p. cm. -- (Opposing Viewpoints)
    Includes bibliographical references and index.
    ISBN-13: 978-0-7377-3333-4 (hardcover lib. : alk. paper)
    ISBN-10: 0-7377-3333-0 (hardcover lib. : alk. paper)
    ISBN-13: 978-0-7377-3334-1 (pbk. : alk. paper)
    ISBN-10: 0-7377-3334-9 (pbk. : alk. paper)
    1. Sexually transmitted diseases--Juvenile literature. 2. Sexually transmitted diseases--Prevention--Juvenile literature. I. Haerens, Margaret. II. Series: Opposing viewpoints series (Unnumbered)
    RC200.25.S48 2007
    616.95'1--dc22

                                                                    2006017067

Printed in the United States of America
10 9 8 7 6 5 4 3 2 1

Contents

Chapter 3: How Can Individuals Reduce the Spread of Sexually Transmitted Diseases?

Chapter 4: How Should the Global AIDS Crisis Be Addressed?

Why Consider Opposing Viewpoints?

> *"The only way in which a human being can make some approach to knowing the whole of a subject is by hearing what can be said about it by persons of every variety of opinion and studying all modes in which it can be looked at by every character of mind. No wise man ever acquired his wisdom in any mode but this."*
>
> John Stuart Mill

In our media-intensive culture it is not difficult to find differing opinions. Thousands of newspapers and magazines and dozens of radio and television talk shows resound with differing points of view. The difficulty lies in deciding which opinion to agree with and which "experts" seem the most credible. The more inundated we become with differing opinions and claims, the more essential it is to hone critical reading and thinking skills to evaluate these ideas. Opposing Viewpoints books address this problem directly by presenting stimulating debates that can be used to enhance and teach these skills. The varied opinions contained in each book examine many different aspects of a single issue. While examining these conveniently edited opposing views, readers can develop critical thinking skills such as the ability to compare and contrast authors' credibility, facts, argumentation styles, use of persuasive techniques, and other stylistic tools. In short, the Opposing Viewpoints Series is an ideal way to attain the higher-level thinking and reading skills so essential in a culture of diverse and contradictory opinions.

In addition to providing a tool for critical thinking, Opposing Viewpoints books challenge readers to question their own strongly held opinions and assumptions. Most people form their opinions on the basis of upbringing, peer pressure, and personal, cultural, or professional bias. By reading carefully balanced opposing views, readers must directly confront new ideas as well as the opinions of those with whom they disagree. This is not to simplistically argue that everyone who reads opposing views will—or should—change his or her opinion. Instead, the series enhances readers' understanding of their own views by encouraging confrontation with opposing ideas. Careful examination of others' views can lead to the readers' understanding of the logical inconsistencies in their own opinions, perspective on why they hold an opinion, and the consideration of the possibility that their opinion requires further evaluation.

Evaluating Other Opinions

To ensure that this type of examination occurs, Opposing Viewpoints books present all types of opinions. Prominent spokespeople on different sides of each issue as well as well-known professionals from many disciplines challenge the reader. An additional goal of the series is to provide a forum for other, less known, or even unpopular viewpoints. The opinion of an ordinary person who has had to make the decision to cut off life support from a terminally ill relative, for example, may be just as valuable and provide just as much insight as a medical ethicist's professional opinion. The editors have two additional purposes in including these less known views. One, the editors encourage readers to respect others' opinions—even when not enhanced by professional credibility. It is only by reading or listening to and objectively evaluating others' ideas that one can determine whether they are worthy of consideration. Two, the inclusion of such viewpoints encourages the important critical thinking skill of objectively evaluating an author's credentials and bias. This evaluation will illuminate an author's reasons for taking a particular stance on an issue and will aid in readers' evaluation of the author's ideas.

It is our hope that these books will give readers a deeper understanding of the issues debated and an appreciation of the complexity of even seemingly simple issues when good and honest people disagree. This awareness is particularly important in a democratic society such as ours in which people enter into public debate to determine the common good. Those with whom one disagrees should not be regarded as enemies but rather as people whose views deserve careful examination and may shed light on one's own.

Thomas Jefferson once said that "difference of opinion leads to inquiry, and inquiry to truth." Jefferson, a broadly educated man, argued that "if a nation expects to be ignorant and free . . . it expects what never was and never will be." As individuals and as a nation, it is imperative that we consider the opinions of others and examine them with skill and discernment. The Opposing Viewpoints Series is intended to help readers achieve this goal.

David L. Bender and Bruno Leone,
Founders

Introduction

"Giving the HPV vaccine to young women could be potentially harmful because they may see it as a license to engage in premarital sex."

—*Bridget Maher,*
Family Research Council

"Public health should be guided by what works. The last thing we need is politicians grandstanding as moralists, because it ends up delivering bad health for young people."

—*James Wagoner,*
Advocates for Youth

The expression of human sexuality has always been influenced by religious ideals and cultural and social mores. Different groups have very different ideas on what sexual behavior is acceptable and how human sexuality should be expressed. In the United States, social and religious conservatives believe in sexual abstinence until marriage and have tried to implement these ideas within school curricula.

Since the election of conservative Republican George W. Bush to the presidency in 2000, social and religious conservatives appointed to powerful and influential positions have been able to shape public health policy to satisfy conservative goals. As a result, funding of abstinence-only sex education increased dramatically. Supporters of abstinence-only education point out that abstinence is the only sure method to protect adolescents from the spread of sexually transmitted diseases (STDs). Critics of this approach charge that students being taught abstinence alone are not getting the information they need about contraception. With the emphasis on abstinence, they claim, studies show that other ways of preventing STD infections are being neglected.

An illustration of this conflict between supporters of the abstinence-only approach to sex education and supporters of a more comprehensive approach is the growing controversy over the recent emergence of a human papillomavirus (HPV) vaccine. One of the most common STDs affecting women today, HPV can often lead to cervical cancer. An estimated 280,000 women die from cervical cancer every year, most of them in the developing world. Each year some ten thousand American women are diagnosed with it; approximately four thousand of them die from it. A new vaccine, called Gardasil, would immunize women against two different types of high risk HPV, HPV-16 and HPV-18, which account for an estimated 70 percent of cervical cancer cases. Even more impressive, the vaccine is reported to be 100 percent effective. Gardasil is considered one of the more significant advances in women's health in the past century.

Public opinion is supportive of the HPV vaccine. A study published in September 2005 in the *Journal of Adolescent Health* reported that up to 80 percent of parents were in favor of having their child vaccinated against treatable, sexually transmitted infections such as HPV. Cancer groups recommend that it become one of the standard vaccines that children, especially girls, receive just before puberty. "I would like to see it that if you don't have your HPV vaccine, you can't start high school," comments Juan Carlos Felix of the University of Southern California, who leads the National Cervical Cancer Coalition's medical advisory panel. For many parents and health-care professionals, the case is clear: If you can immunize your child against a potential cancer threat, you should do it.

However, some social and religious conservatives are not as enthusiastic about the HPV vaccine. To them, making the HPV vaccine mandatory for young women would be equivalent to condoning sexual activity before marriage. According to Reginald Finger, a doctor and member of the Advisory Committee on Immunization Practices, a panel of experts brought together by the Centers for Disease Control and Prevention, "There are people who sense that it could cause people to feel like sexual behaviors are safer if they are vaccinated and may lead to more sexual behavior because they feel safe." The success of the HPV vaccine is viewed as a threat to the abstinence-only message for adolescents. The Family Research Council's Tony Perkins contends that immunization sends the wrong message. "Our concern is that this vaccine will be marketed to a segment of the population that should be getting a message about abstinence."

However, other conservatives argue that practical health concerns should come before religious ideals. Bill Frisbie, director of campus ministry at the University of Texas at Austin, asserts that "the health benefits [of the vaccine] would far outweigh possible concerns people might have about promiscuity." Other supporters of the HPV vaccine concur, arguing that immunizing young girls is not encouraging them to engage in premarital sex—it is protecting them from a virulent cancer and saving lives. Alan Kaye, executive director of the National Cervical Cancer Coalition, sees parallels between the vaccine and wearing a seat belt. "Just because you wear a seat belt doesn't mean you're seeking out an accident," Kaye says.

The viewpoints presented in *Opposing Viewpoints: Sexually Transmitted Diseases* explore the conflict between social conservatives and progressives over sex education and STD-prevention programs in the following chapters: Are Sexually Transmitted Diseases a Serious Problem? How Should the Government Educate Youths About Sexually Transmitted

Diseases? How Can Individuals Reduce the Spread of Sexually Transmitted Diseases? How Should the Global AIDS Crisis Be Addressed? The information in this volume will provide insight into the political, social, and cultural dimensions of fighting sexually transmitted diseases.

CHAPTER 1

Are Sexually Transmitted Diseases a Serious Problem?

Chapter Preface

The actual incidence and rate of infection of sexually transmitted diseases (STDs) is difficult to measure: Even reliable estimates can vary widely when individuals are either reluctant to report signs of infection or, as is often the case, when there are no apparent signs of infection. A 1988 report by the Centers for Disease Control and Prevention (CDC) estimated that there are 12 million new STD infections each year. A December 1998 report by the Kaiser Family Foundation calculates that there are approximately 15 million new infections annually. Yet even those numbers may be low. If people do not get tested, no diagnoses can be made. Moreover, only a few STDs—gonorrhea, syphilis, and chlamydia—are reported on a national level to the CDC. Therefore, there is limited data on other major STDs such as genital herpes, hepatitis B, and human papilloma virus.

With all of these factors complicating the tracking of STDs, measuring their incidence is challenging. The Kaiser Family Foundation claims that "the true number of new infections could be as low as 10 million or as high as 20 million a year." It is also difficult to determine whether STD rates are decreasing or increasing. Experts note that infection rates for some STDs have decreased, especially some bacterial STDs like chlamydia, gonorrhea, and syphilis. Overall rates of HIV have also held stable. Yet in some instances rates for some STDs— such as HIV among African Americans and syphilis among gay men—are on the rise again.

On a global level, the monitoring of STDs (including HIV/ AIDS) is done by the World Health Organization (WHO) and UNAIDS. The goal of this collaboration is to compile the best information available and to improve the quality of data on national, regional, and global levels. As in the United States, international organizations strive to provide the most accurate statistics on STD infections because these numbers affect social and political policies as well as funding decisions for programs and health care. In addition, estimates influence public perception as to how serious the problem of STD infections is and what resources should be allocated to fight it.

The following chapter presents viewpoints that explore the extent of STD incidence. Some authors argue that STDs are a serious problem, while others contend that the incidence of these diseases has been exaggerated.

| "The numbers associated with [the
| STD] epidemic are simply staggering."

STDs Are a Serious Problem

The Youth Connection

In the following viewpoint, the Youth Connection, *a publication of the Institute for Youth Development, provides statistics that show an alarming rise in the prevalence of sexually transmitted diseases (STDs), particularly among American youth. The authors identify human papilloma virus (HPV), herpes type 2, and HIV/AIDS as especially threatening. The Institute for Youth Development is a nonprofit organization that promotes a comprehensive risk-avoidance message regarding alcohol, drugs, sex, tobacco, and violence among children and adolescents.*

As you read, consider the following questions:

1. According to the authors, what two false perceptions contribute to the lack of media attention to the STD epidemic among young people?
2. According to a June 2000 Institute of Allergy and Infectious Diseases report cited by the *Youth Connection,* how many Americans have been infected with an STD?

The Youth Connection, "STDs: A Teenage Epidemic?" vol. 5, March-April, 2004, pp. 3–5. Reproduced by permission of the Institute for Youth Development.

3. *STD* is a general term, the authors explain, that covers how many different sexually transmitted diseases?

Twenty-five years ago, who would have thought that teenage sex could have life-threatening consequences? Not that an unwanted pregnancy or an STD such as gonorrhea or syphilis that was prevalent then isn't a tremendous challenge to a teenager's life, but the stakes are now much higher.

In some ways, we are experiencing a silent invasion. There are no huge headlines on magazine covers and no public service initiatives to highlight the increasingly serious threat facing our teens.

For many of us, this has occurred because of two false perceptions. The first is that there are a limited number of STDs out there, and that apart from HIV/AIDS, few, if any, are life-threatening. The second is that as long as we practice "safe sex" we are indeed safe.

Nothing could be further from the truth.

The Numbers Speak for Themselves

The numbers associated with this epidemic are simply staggering. In June, 2000, the National Institutes of Health's Institute of Allergy and Infectious Diseases reported that more than 65 million people in the U.S. are living with an STD—the majority of which are incurable viral infections. That's nearly 25% of the U.S. population, and the number continues to grow.

The numbers seem to be increasing. During the year 2000, approximately 18.9 million new cases of STD occurred, with young people aged 15–24 accounting for 9.1 million cases. Interestingly enough, these numbers may be conservative because not all teens experience symptoms and therefore are not diagnosed and counted.

Some researchers believe that as many as 80% of teens with STDs never seek medical attention because they do not notice or recognize symptoms. A study of teen girls who had

one or more infections of herpes, chlamydia, gonorrhea, syphilis, and hepatitis B indicated that 87% did not exhibit symptoms. Some teens who do experience symptoms may choose not to be treated because of fear or embarrassment.

Not only is the number of infections large and growing, so are the types of STDs.

Types of STDs

For starters, STD is short-hand for somewhere between 25 and 50 different types of sexually-transmitted diseases. Diseases that are caused by sexually-transmitted infections range from irritating but treatable to life threatening

In addition to the more well-known STDs such as syphilis, chlamydia, herpes, and gonorrhea, there are new viral strains that are not talked about in the mainstream press and are, therefore, not well known. Overall, viruses are particularly troublesome because they are incurable. Once you've contracted a virus, it's up to the immune system to suppress it or allow it to grow. Viruses are spreading like wildfire.

HPV

The human papilloma virus (HPV) is a potentially deadly disease that is incurable. There are more than 100 different strains in existence today. HPV is directly linked to 99.7% of all cervical cancer. HPV-related cancer kills more women in the U.S. today than HIV/AIDS.

In 2000, HPV infection accounted for approximately 6.2 million of all sexually-transmitted diseases among Americans aged 15–44. It is estimated that 74% occurred among 15–24-year-olds. It also accounts for 45% of the total medical cost for all STDs in the U.S. The total annual STD cost in the U.S. is estimated to be $6.5 billion.

A variety of studies have shown that after their first sexual contact, girls have a 46% chance of contracting HPV. A recent study revealed that 50% of sexually-active females between 18

**Approximate number of Americans
affected by STDs each year**

STD	Number affected
Chlamydia	4 million
Trichomoniasis ("trich")	3 million
Gonorrhea ("clap")	1.1 million
Genital Warts (HBV)	750,000
Genital Herpes	40 million affected, with as many as 500,000 new cases each year
Hepatitis B	300,00
Syphilis ("syph")	120
HIV	1 million affected, with as many as 45,00 new AIDS cases reported each year

SOURCE: American Social Health Association, 2005.

and 22 have HPV. Gynecologists throughout the country are reporting that they are seeing an alarming number of pre-cancerous conditions among girls who are in their teens and early 20s.

Herpes Type 2

Equally alarming is that approximately 20% of our population over the age of 12 has the herpes type 2 virus. The U.S. Centers for Disease Control and Prevention believe the number could be as large as 45 million+ people. There has been a 500% increase in herpes type 2 in white teens since 1976. It is estimated that teens aged 15–24 acquire 640,000 new herpes type 2 infections each year. Herpes type 2 causes genital infections, but it can also infect the mouth. Symptoms can be treated, but like HPV, it is an incurable virus that retreats into the nerve cells and then randomly recurs—sometimes with great frequency.

Herpes type 2 is very contagious. While most people become infected when the other partner is having an outbreak, it is believed that the virus can shed cells in between outbreaks, thereby causing infections when no symptoms are present.

Overall, herpes can be a very painful, disruptive, and psychologically damaging disease for teens, their future mates and their unborn children. In addition to uncomfortable outbreaks, a female who has a first episode of herpes type 2 while pregnant can pass it along to her baby. This can cause premature births, nerve damage, and other serious problems that affect the brain, skin and eyes of the child.

HIV/AIDS

And then, there's HIV/AIDS. While most people are familiar with this disease, it is not widely known that a person can be infected and contagious before a blood test detects the antibodies that are present as a result of the virus. This should be a very sobering fact for teens and adults alike as they make decisions about whether they should engage in sexual relationships.

> *"We are winning the battle [against STDs]. . . . We've seen . . . dramatic declines [in infection rates.]"*

The Threat of STDs Is Exaggerated

Alison Motluck

In the following viewpoint, Alison Motluck argues that sexually transmitted diseases (STDs) are less of a threat than in years past. In fact, she maintains, there have been several successes in the war against STDs, and she cites the decreasing rates of syphilis and chlamydia in the United States. She goes on to discuss a few emerging technologies that she views as significant breakthroughs in the fight to reduce rates of STDs around the world. Motluck is a reporter for New Scientist, *a British science magazine.*

As you read, consider the following questions:

1. Why does the author believe STDs are not as big a problem as in the past?

2. What does Motluck recommend to further reduce STD rates?

3. What are some promising breakthroughs in the fight against STDs, according to the author?

That famous British reserve all but disappeared [the week of March 9, 2002,] as warnings spread like wildfire that sexually transmitted diseases were on the increase, and that if they continued unchecked the country faced a public health disaster. National newspapers stoked the fires of moral indignation, and the British Medical Association even recommended that school-children as young as five should be lectured about the dangers of unsafe sex.

The debate was sparked by two rather mundane studies, both published in the journal *Sexually Transmitted Infections*. One found that people nowadays are more accepting of casual and gay sex, and the other showed that people with STDs, especially men, are reluctant to tell their partners that they may have put them at risk. By the end of the week, the public was expected to believe that Britain is in the grip of an epidemic of STDs fuelled by lax sexual attitudes.

But are STDs really more of a threat now than ever? A glance backwards at the 20th century suggests that the grandparents and parents of today's supposedly licentious youth lived in much more dangerous times. According to Britain's Public Health Laboratory Service (PHLS), gonorrhoea was over three times as prevalent as today after the Second World War and about four times as common in the late 1960s and early 1970s. These days syphilis barely registers on the charts, whereas after the war, tens of thousands of cases were being reported each year. Even genital herpes infection rates have remained flat in recent years. And most public health officials admit that much of the apparent increase in chlamydia is simply due to better detection.

"There have been lots of successes," says Kevin Fenton of University College London and the PHLS. "In general, we are winning the battle." Since 1995, there have been disturbing outbreaks of syphilis and gonorrhoea in isolated communities across Britain. But while the problem is serious, Fenton says it has to be viewed in context. "It's all relative," he says. "We've seen such dramatic declines."

STDs in the United States

The situation is similar in the US, where syphilis is at an all-time low—so low that the US Centers for Disease Control and Prevention in Atlanta has concluded that it could be eradicated. Though there was a small increase in rates of gonorrhoea in the late 1990s, infections went down by 10 per cent a year in the decade preceding that rise. There is no evidence that there are fewer cases of genital warts, but chlamydia is thought to be declining.

Everyone agrees that there's no excuse for complacency. Even the STDs that don't kill can cause considerable suffering. Untreated, chlamydia can cause pelvic inflammatory disease, which can lead to infertility, for instance. And some types of human papillomavirus, which produce genital warts, lead to cervical, penile and anal cancers.

The British Medical Association has called for more sex education and public health campaigns. But education can only do so much. The most effective way to reduce rates of STDs may lie in better screening, including faster, easier and cheaper tests, and more options for protection than condoms alone.

Many STDs, such as syphilis, gonorrhoea and chlamydia, are bacterial, and are easily treated with antibiotics. Yet often they go undiagnosed, increasing the chances of being passed on. "There's a huge misconception out there that people who have STDs will know it," says Edward Hook at the University

The New Sexual Hysteria

Go online for information about moles, and it's not hard to convince yourself you've got skin cancer. Out of breath after a workout? You can quickly match up your symptoms with adult-onset asthma. Feeling clumsy and uncoordinated? Better get checked for MS. The Internet is like oxygen to a hypochondriac's fire, turning general anxiety into a full-blown, life-altering obsession. "People pick up fragmented information," explains Zachary Bregman, an internist and assistant clinical professor at the Albert Einstein College of Medicine. "There is an increasing degree of hypochondria among young people in general. If it was something I saw in 2 or 3 percent of people before, I'm seeing it in 6 percent now." And most of the hypochondriacs, says Bregman, are fixated on STDs—diseases so personal and stigmatized that they lend themselves to private, panicky surf sessions. The millions of sexual-health sites, with their warnings and statistics and symptoms, are daunting even in a sober state of mind. But after a night of intoxicated sex and a burning sensation upon urination, a Web search can lead to an unqualified diagnosis, paranoia, and a sharp shift—temporary or permanent—in sexual behavior.

Grant Stoddard, New York Metro, *November 22, 2004.*

of Alabama in Birmingham. But many don't: often they have no symptoms, or ignore them. "We're all masters of denial," he says.

The only way to address that problem is through screening, says Hook. In the US, federal guidelines encourage the screening of high-risk populations—for instance, testing all sexually active women under 24 for chlamydia. But the guidelines are not always acted on. Similarly, people in Britain are only screened once they attend a genitourinary medicine clinic. However, Fenton believes that screening the general population will be introduced in Britain within the next decade.

Advances in testing methods have already made widespread screening much more practical. There are now four or five rapid tests for STDs that amplify signature amino acids in a urine sample. "They are all more sensitive than the old gold standards," says Hook. And although the cost is still prohibitive for some, the tests avoid the embarrassment and discomfort of a swab. All you need to do is pee into a cup.

Safe Sex

Sexual behaviour is still a very strong determinant of STD rates, says Fenton. Having many partners, not using condoms and having gay sex all increase a person's chance of contracting an STD. But Fenton admits there aren't a lot of options for people who want to practise safe sex.

"We've been singing the same condom mantra for fifty years," says Sharon Hillier at the University of Pittsburgh School of Medicine. "The problem with condoms is not their effectiveness but that they're not used." She researches "microbicides"—topical products that aim to prevent the transmission of HIV and other STD pathogens. There are no microbicides on the market yet, but three are about to begin clinical trials.

Though less effective than condoms, microbicides may end up protecting more people from STDs, simply because people may be more willing to use them, says Megan Gottemoeller of the Program for Appropriate Technology in Health, based in Washington, DC. But there's little scientific or commercial interest in these products as they don't rely on cutting-edge science and won't make big money early on. And policymakers "want to fix this epidemic without mentioning 'sex' or 'vagina'", she says.

Another promising front is vaccination. Vaccines against human papilloma virus and HIV are in phase II and phase III trials respectively in the US. Other vaccines against chlamydia are in earlier stages of development. So far, only the herpes vaccine has proved effective—providing about 75 per cent protection—but it doesn't work in men.

Ideally, all prepubescent girls would receive the anti-herpes jab. But it might be difficult to persuade parents to get their daughters vaccinated, and could stir up an intense moral and scientific debate in its own right. "There's some concern that if you give kids an STD vaccine, it will give them permission to go out and have sex," says Susan Rosenthal, a psychologist at the University of Texas Medical Branch in Galveston. She feels that's unlikely, but says the vaccine will only work if it is routinely given to all girls.

| "Armies of troops in Central Africa are being depleted—not by rockets and machine guns, but by AIDS."

The AIDS Epidemic Is Devastating Africa

Patrick Dixon

In the following viewpoint, Patrick Dixon describes the extent of the AIDS epidemic in Africa. He argues that the virus has brought devastation to African families and entire communities. Dixon is the chairman of Global Change Ltd., a global forecasting company, and the author of several books on such subjects as AIDS, genetics, and drugs.

As you read, consider the following questions:

1. By 2002, how many Africans had been infected with the AIDS virus, according to Dixon?
2. According to the author, how many African countries have AIDS prevalence rates over 20 percent?
3. In the author's opinion, what are some of the challenges

Patrick Dixon, "The Extent of the AIDS Nightmare," *The Truth about AIDS*, 2002. Reproduced by permission.

of educating Africans about HIV/AIDS and its prevention?

Unless something changes, over 250 million people will die from AIDS in the next few years. We are still in the earliest stages of the epidemic. The spread of HIV across the globe is [in 2002] twice as fast as five years ago, with 85 million infected by the end of 2002. We appear to be losing the battle in many of the poorest nations, yet there is an answer. . . .

It was 1981. In a Los Angeles doctor's office the men sitting in white coats were worried: within a few weeks they had diagnosed their fourth case of a condition so incredibly rare they had hardly expected to see it in their collective professional lifetime. They were baffled by the series of strange pneumonias that got worse despite normal antibiotics. All of the patients were men. All were young. All of them had died.

Three and a half thousand miles to the east, at a hospital in New York, several doctors were faced with a similar problem: strange tumours and lethal pneumonias in young men. What was going on?

The cases were all reported to the infectious disease centre. Could this be some sort of epidemic? Were the pneumonias and cancers caused by the same thing? What did the men have in common? Every day new reports of deaths came flooding in. It was becoming clear that most, if not all, of the deceased were men who had had sex with other men. The disease quickly became labelled 'the gay plague'. How wrong they would turn out to be.

Dozens of strange infections were seen—with all the classic signs of weakened natural defences. The disease was called AIDS—Acquired Immune Deficiency Syndrome. It took some time to discover that the culprit was a tiny virus, called the Human Immunodeficiency Virus, or HIV. It is now known that someone can be infected with HIV for ten years or more before developing the illness called AIDS.

A Growing Epidemic

Just five years later, by November 1986, 15,345 people had already died, another 12,000 were dying, and a further 30,000 were feeling unwell.

People were concerned that maybe up to a million people in the United States were also infected but were not yet ill. At first the 'experts' predicted only one in ten of those infected would die, then two in ten, then three in ten, then nine out of ten. Now we know that almost everyone with the infection will die as a result.

Most estimates from the early 1980s were exceeded. By April 1990 in the United States there were over 126,000 cases reported. (There were estimates of possibly 200–300,000 feeling unwell and maybe 700,000 infected, representing up to one in sixty of all men in the United States between the ages of twenty and fifty. In New York, AIDS became the commonest cause of death for men and women aged twenty-five to forty-four, with 100 AIDS deaths every week. One in every sixty-one babies carried HIV. By 1993 more people were dying of AIDS in the United States each year than died in the entire ten-year Vietnam War—compared to 6,000 deaths total in the UK. By 2002 over 45,000 American citizens were still being infected every year, despite 15 years of prevention campaign.

The number of people already doomed in the United States made the Vietnam tragedy look like a minor skirmish, with one new infection every thirteen minutes. The coffins, if placed end to end, would stretch for 1,000 miles.

Yet while all the attention at first was on America, another similar but far more catastrophic disaster was silently destroying another continent, and no one had noticed.

The African Experience

Some years after AIDS was first diagnosed in the United States, the first cases were recognised in Africa. We know today that

The AIDS Crisis in Africa

People with AIDS don't suffer alone—the disease attacks their families and communities as well. AIDS has stripped out an entire generation of parents, farmers, doctors, leaders. 12 million African children have already lost one or both parents to AIDS, and unless we take serious action now, there will be more than 18 million AIDS orphans by the end of the decade. Millions of children will have lost not only their parents, but their teachers, nurses and friends, too. Businesses are losing their workers, governments are losing their civil servants, families are losing their breadwinners. As a result, entire communities are devastated and economies that are already crippled by poverty, debts and unfair trade policies are further compromised.

"The AIDS Crisis," Data.org, 2005. www.data.org.

for years thousands had been dying, but their deaths were blamed on tuberculosis and other diseases.

In many towns and cities across Central Africa, up to a third of all young adults are infected. A third of the truck drivers running the main north/south routes and half the prostitutes in many towns are carrying HIV. One relief agency in the early 1990s talked unofficially about pulling out of Central Africa. 'What's the point in drilling more wells when most of the people will be dead in a few years?'

Over 45 million Africans were infected by 2002 of which more than 30 million were still alive. A further 12 million children had already lost one or both of their parents. The effects over the last 15 years have been a catastrophe. Seven countries, all in southern Africa, now have prevalence rates higher than 20%: Botswana (38.8%), Lesotho (31%), Namibia

(22.5%), South Africa (20.1%), Swaziland (33.4%), Zambia (21.5%) and Zimbabwe (33.7%).

Uganda remains the only country to have subdued a major HIV/AIDS epidemic, with the adult HIV prevalence rate continuing to drop—from 8.3% at the end of 1999 to 5% at the end of 2001. Huge challenges persist, however, such as taking care of the 880,000 Ugandan children who have been orphaned by AIDS. 60% of all adults infected are women.

A First-Hand Account

I have visited villages where grandmothers are looking after their grandchildren because so many young men and women, the parents, have been wiped out by AIDS. Armies of troops in Central Africa are being depleted—not by rockets and machine guns, but by AIDS. Breadwinners for families and providers of the countries' wealth are missing. The educated elite living in the main towns and cities have often been worst hit.

In the country, fields are uncultivated and cattle wander aimlessly. One journalist visiting an African country described areas where whole families had been wiped out, plantations gone back to bush. I have met someone who claims to have satellite photographs of a country in Central Africa taken two years apart, showing not deforestation, but reforestation as the amount of farming falls. It is an effect attributed to AIDS—the country is not at war.

As early as 1991 I found it hard in a city like Kampala [Uganda] to find a family that was not attending an AIDS funeral on average once a month. Deaths continued to soar over the next decade among young adults. In Africa they called it the 'slim' disease. Some Africans believe if you sleep with only fat women you are safe. 'To be fat is to be healthy.' Uganda has seen a dramatic response to prevention campaigns but for those already infected it is all too late.

In the early days of the pandemic, officials stood at the doors of some hospitals selecting the fit ones for treatment. Anyone who looked thin and weak was sent back into the bush—'Probably got AIDS; nothing we can do for him.' Many were sent away with perfectly treatable diseases such as tuberculosis. You cannot tell the difference at the door.

Years and years of careful preventive medicine has been undermined. How do you start educating about a disease which produces no illness for years, when nurses are still battling against ingrained habits just to get mothers to give their children a healthy diet?

The children's wards are full of dying children. Many are babies under one or two years old. Many are not dying of famine, but of AIDS. A terrible tragedy is that a significant number in the 1980s and early 1990s caught the virus not while in their mothers' wombs, or from their mother's milk, but from the use of unsterilised needles.

AIDS is not a gay plague; there are millions more women and children infected with HIV throughout the world than there are gay men. It gained this reputation in the United States because gay men were first to be diagnosed, yet 98% of all new infections worldwide are heterosexually acquired—and in the poorest nations.

> "AIDS is not, as many believe, Africa's
> primary health threat; . . . In fact,
> AIDS is not the leading cause of illness
> or death in any African country."

AIDS Is Not the Cause of Africa's Health Crisis

Christine Maggiore

In the following viewpoint, Christine Maggiore questions the prevailing notion that there is an AIDS epidemic in Africa. Challenging the methods of diagnosing AIDS in Africa, she argues that cases of dysentery, malnutrition, and parasitic infections, all endemic problems in Africa, may be misdiagnosed as AIDS. Thus, the rate of AIDS transmission may be much lower than reported by international health organizations. Maggiore is the founder of Alive & Well AIDS Alternatives, an organization that challenges the accuracy of HIV tests, the safety and effectiveness of AIDS drug treatments, and the validity of most common assumptions about HIV and AIDS.

As you read, consider the following questions:

Christine Maggiore, *What If Everything You Thought You Knew About AIDS Was Wrong, Revised 4th Edition*, Studio City, CA: The American Foundation for AIDS Alternatives, 2006. © 2006. Reproduced by permission.

1. According to the author, how does the method of diagnosing AIDS in Africa differ from the diagnostic methods in the United States?

2. What is the relationship between SIV and HIV, according to Maggiore?

3. Why does the author believe that there are significant problems with HIV testing in Africa?

According to the 1999 World Health Organization (WHO) report, the total number of actual diagnosed AIDS cases on the African continent is about equal to the total for AIDS in America even though Africa, with its 650 million people, has more than two times the population of the USA. Africa is often cited as a worst case example of what could happen in America despite figures that demonstrate that 99.5% of Africans do not have AIDS, and among Africans who test HIV positive, 97% do not have AIDS.

Unlike in the United States, AIDS in Africa may be diagnosed based on four clinical symptoms—fever, involuntary loss of 10% of normal body weight, persistent cough, and diarrhea—and HIV tests are not required. The four clinical AIDS symptoms are identical to those associated with conditions that run rampant on the African continent such as malaria, tuberculosis, parasitic infections, the effects of malnutrition, and unsanitary drinking and bathing water. These symptoms are the result of poverty and other problems that have troubled Africa and other developing areas of the world for many decades.

The idea that AIDS originated in Africa remains popular although there has never been scientific or epidemiological evidence to substantiate this notion. News reports suggesting that HIV began in Africa as Simian Immunodeficiency Virus (SIV) are based on elaborate speculation about species-jumping viruses rather than reliable evidence.

Are the Numbers Misleading?

A growing number of researchers question the "official" inflated numbers of HIV/AIDS prevalence in African countries such as Botswana, South Africa and Lesotho. Poor testing, a special diagnosis of AIDS in Africa and erroneous computer-generated estimates by the [United Nations] had led to "misleading" numbers, they hold.

Rainer Hennig, Afrol News, *2004.*
www.afrol.com.

SIV induces only flulike symptoms in some experimental laboratory monkeys and does not cause any of the 29 official AIDS-defining illnesses. Unlike HIV infection, which is said to cause illness only years after exposure and despite the presence of protective antibodies, SIV will cause illness within days of infection or not at all, and wild monkeys retain SIV antibodies throughout their lives without ever becoming ill. Only monkeys in unnatural circumstances—lab animals with undeveloped immune systems who are injected with large quantities of SIV—become ill.

In a recent attempt to advance the hypothesis of an SIV/HIV connection. researchers used the results of nonspecific antibody tests to claim that three chimpanzees captured in West Africa had been infected with HIV/SIV through sexual transmission. Efforts to isolate actual virus from the animals revealed that two of the three chimps had no virus, while the researchers admitted that the virus found in the one was not even closely related to HIV. Their report also failed to explain why the "infected" animals did not transmit HIV/SIV to any of the 150 other chimps living in the colony where they were kept, or why their mates and offspring did not test positive.

While Africa is the frequent subject of dramatic media reports, actual numbers of diagnosed AIDS cases on the continent are relatively unremarkable. For example, 1981 through 1999 cumulative AIDS cases for South Africa, the new epicenter of AIDS, total just 12,825.

Unfounded estimates, rather than unprotected sex, are responsible for the alarming number of AIDS cases said to occur in Africa. United Nations' AIDS estimates were cited as the inspiration for a recent news report claiming "a Kenyan dies of AIDS every three minutes." If Kenyans were dying at this rate, there would be more than twice as many dead Kenyans in just one year than have ever been actually diagnosed with AIDS in the entire period of time known as the AIDS epidemic.

In 1987, the WHO estimated there were 1 million HIV positives in Uganda, the nation then considered the epicenter of AIDS. Ten years later, WHO estimates for Uganda remained unchanged at 1 million HIV positives while the total of actual AIDS cases through 1999 are less than 55,000 in this country of more than 20 million people.

AIDS is not, as many believe, Africa's primary health threat; several million cases of tuberculosis and malaria are reported each year in Africa while total AIDS cases on the continent for the entire AIDS epidemic hover just above one-half million. For example, in 1996 there were 170,000 cases of tuberculosis reported in Ethiopia and less than 850 cases of AIDS; South Africa's tuberculosis cases topped 91,000 compared to 729 diagnosed cases of AIDS. In fact, AIDS is not the leading cause of illness or death in any African country.

Because of the high incidence of exposure to malaria, tuberculosis and other diseases that produce false-positive results on HIV tests, many mainstream scientists question the validity of HIV testing in Africa.

> "Syphilis rates rose dramatically for the
> second straight year in the United
> States . . . [and] this probably is only
> the tip of the iceberg."

Syphilis Is a Growing Threat

Steve Mitchell

*In the following viewpoint, Steve Mitchell describes a disturbing
rise in the rate of syphilis infections in the United States,
particularly among gay men, and notes that several other
countries have reported a similar increase in syphilis rates. According to Mitchell, a rise in syphilis rates is dangerous because
the genital sores caused by syphilis make it easier to transmit
and to become infected with HIV. Mitchell is the medical cor-
respondent for United Press International, a newswire service.*

As you read, consider the following questions:

1. How much did the syphilis rate rise from 2000–2001,
   according to Mitchell?
2. According to the author, why are syphilis rates increasing among gay men?
3. How does the CDC plan to combat the rise in syphilis
   rates, according to the author?

Syphilis rates [in 2002] rose dramatically for the second straight year in the United States, particularly among gay and bisexual men, a finding that has health officials worried about an increase in HIV/AIDS cases in the coming years.

Overall, the U.S. syphilis rate rose by 9 percent between 2001 and 2002, the second consecutive increase from an all-time low in 2000, according to figures released by the Centers for Disease Control and Prevention [CDC] in Atlanta.

The bulk of the increase occurred among men, rising by about 27 percent overall, including a staggering increase of more than 85 percent among white men and a nearly 36 percent increase among Latino men. Information on sexual orientation is often not collected by health departments, but the CDC estimates 40 percent of the increase was in gay and bisexual men.

The total number of syphilis cases increased from 6,100 to more than 6,800, but CDC officials think this probably is only the tip of the iceberg because many cases go undiagnosed.

"The overall number is probably significantly higher," Dr. John Douglas, director of the CDC's division of sexually transmitted diseases, said during a teleconference about the new figures, which appear in the Nov. 21 [2003] issue of CDC's *Morbidity and Mortality Weekly Report.*

The rise in syphilis infections indicates a growing number of gay and bisexual men are having unprotected sex, which worries health officials because the men could be spreading other diseases, including HIV/AIDS.

Increases in Other Countries

The problem is not just limited to the United States. "Several other countries, including the United Kingdom, the Netherlands, Australia and several countries in western Europe have also reported increases of syphilis and other diseases among gay and bisexual men and in many of these there are high levels of HIV co-infection," said Dr. Ronald O. Valdiserri, deputy director of CDC's HIV, sexually transmitted diseases and tuberculosis prevention center.

Valdiserri said there is no clear evidence HIV cases are increasing yet in the United States, "but we are extremely concerned about that possibility."

He noted a study released in July [2003] at the National HIV Prevention Conference in Atlanta found rates of diagnosis with HIV infection were up by 17 percent among men who have sex with men. This does not necessarily represent new cases, however, so it is difficult to determine if the HIV infection rate actually is increasing, "but we're very concerned about that increase because it wasn't observed in other risk groups," Valdiserri said.

Heightening concern further is the fact that syphilis increases the risk of HIV transmission by two to five times, because the genital sores caused by syphilis serve as portals of entry for the AIDS virus, Douglas said. In addition, a recent study found HIV viral load increases when a person has syphilis, suggesting he or she may be more contagious.

Sue Blank, assistant commissioner at the Bureau of Sexually Transmitted Disease Control at the New York City Department of Health and Mental Hygiene, said she is worried about syphilis increases—with 434 cases in 2002, New York had the most of any U.S. city—because they could translate into an increase in HIV/AIDS infections.

"Certainly, the concern for us is the syphilis outbreaks are going to be heralding increases in HIV," Blank said.

Prevention Strategies

The CDC is now mobilizing efforts to battle the syphilis problem and officials are confident that prevention strategies can help keep the disease in check. Although syphilis increased in gay and bisexual men, education and intensified testing efforts appear to have resulted in a decline in cases among African-American men and a 19-percent drop among women

What Is the Link Between Syphilis and HIV?

Genital sores (chancres) caused by syphilis make it easier to transmit and acquire HIV infection sexually. There is an estimated 2- to 5-fold increased risk of acquiring HIV infection when syphilis is present.

Ulcerative STDs that cause sores, ulcers, or breaks in the skin or mucous membranes, such as syphilis, disrupt barriers that provide protection against infections. The genital ulcers caused by syphilis can bleed easily, and when they come into contact with oral and rectal mucosa during sex, increase the infectiousness of and susceptibility to HIV. Having other STDs is also an important predictor for becoming HIV infected because STDs are a marker for behaviors associated with HIV transmission.

Centers for Disease Control and Prevention,
"Syphilis & MSM Fact Sheet," 2005.
www.cdc.gov.

overall—including nearly a 22-percent decrease in African-American females.

However, prevention strategies will need to be tailored to the gay community to keep the disease in check in that population, Valdiserri said.

Although the factors driving the increase among gay and bisexual men are "multi-factorial"—not due to one single cause—some of the reasons include a relaxed attitude about sexually transmitted diseases. This is due to the introduction of medications that can keep AIDS in check, Valdiserri said. Other reasons include substance abuse and "emerging venues that facilitate unprotected sex, including the Internet," he added.

Blank noted when her department interviewed a number of gay and bisexual men in 2002 about their sexual habits, it found recruiting sexual partners over the Internet was a common practice, including among those infected with syphilis.

Blank's group also found, however, men infected with syphilis were much more likely to report HIV infection than those not infected with syphilis. In addition, syphilis-infected men were more likely to report unprotected anal intercourse, attending private sex parties, use of illicit drugs and 11 or more partners in the past six months.

Getting the Word Out

One of the strategies CDC intends to employ is to encourage organizations that serve gay and bisexual men to get the word out about the importance of detecting and treating syphilis.

Paul Feldman of the National Association of People with AIDS in Washington, said his organization would be willing to work with the CDC. But he noted a larger problem is a lack of funding for HIV and sexually transmitted disease prevention efforts.

For the fiscal year 2004 budget, the [George W.] Bush administration requested a reduction of $9 million in the funds for CDC's HIV prevention and surveillance efforts, Feldman said. "Decreasing it in a time when an epidemic rages is insulting and frightening," he said.

The administration also requested decreasing the CDC's budget for prevention of sexually transmitted diseases, which already barely registers at a scant $168 million for the entire country for 2003.

The syphilis rise and potential increases in AIDS cases will cause untold increases in lost wages, healthcare costs and human suffering, Feldman said. All of this easily could "be ameliorated with additional money," he said.

"We have the tools and resources at hand to effectively eliminate syphilis in the United States."

The Eradication of Syphilis Is Within Reach

Judy Wasserheit and George Counts

In the following viewpoint, Judy Wasserheit and George Counts underscore the recent decrease of syphilis and congenital syphilis infections across all socioeconomic levels. They contend that the elimination of the disease is possible with five critical strategies: strengthening community development and partnership, developing rapid response plans, improving access to timely clinical and laboratory services, implementing effective health campaigns, and tracking and monitoring syphilis. Wasserheit is director of the Division of STD Prevention of the Centers for Disease Control and Prevention (CDC). Counts directs the CDC's syphilis elimination efforts.

As you read, consider the following questions:

1. When did the last syphilis epidemic peak in the United States, according to Wasserheit?

Judy Wasserheit and George Counts, "Syphilis Overview" http://www.cdc.gov/std/press/ talkptcsyph7–2001.htm, July 12, 2001. Reproduced by permission.

2. How does Wasserheit define "syphilis elimination?"

3. According to Counts, what percentage of congenital syphilis infections will result in infant deaths?

Judy Wasserheit: The last U.S. syphilis epidemic peaked in 1990, with the highest syphilis rates in 40 years. Although infections have subsided since then to the lowest level since reporting began, history shows that syphilis rates tend to run in seven to 10 year cycles. Unless we take action to eliminate it now, we could once again experience a rise in syphilis rates.

Thankfully, we have the tools and resources at hand to effectively eliminate syphilis in the United States. Syphilis is easily diagnosed and cured, given adequate access to and utilization of care. The challenge is to ensure that all Americans are able to benefit from syphilis treatment.

Today, syphilis disproportionately affects African Americans living in poverty, primarily in the South and in selected urban areas. For these communities, the consequences of syphilis are severe: increased likelihood of HIV transmission and compromises to infant health, resulting from the transmission of syphilis from mother to child. Eliminating syphilis in the United States would be a landmark achievement. It would significantly improve the well being of women and infants, decrease one of the most glaring racial disparities in health and reduce HIV transmission in the United States.

Eliminating Syphilis

Let me take a moment to define what we mean when we talk about syphilis elimination:

- Syphilis elimination is the absence of sustained transmission in the United States. This means that, while there may be occasional outbreaks, these outbreaks can be quickly identified and contained, eliminating the risk of a new epidemic.

- Our national goal, therefore, is to reduce infectious

syphilis cases to 1,000 or fewer annually, and to increase the number of syphilis-free counties to at least 90%. . . . The data that Dr. Counts will discuss [below] represent an important step toward our national goal of syphilis elimination. . . .

In 1998, CDC initiated a national effort to eliminate syphilis in the United States. The fact that we had the lowest syphilis rates in U.S. history and the geographic concentration of disease provided an opportunity to build on current STD [sexually transmitted disease] prevention and control efforts to combine intensified traditional approaches with innovative new ones. Five strategies are critical to this effort:

- Foremost among these is strengthened community involvement and partnership. Because syphilis is highly localized, CDC is working closely with community partners and state and local governments to strengthen programs in hardest-hit communities.

- CDC is also working with the appropriate authorities at local and state levels to develop rapid response plans in the event of a syphilis outbreak.

- Through our expanded partnerships, CDC is helping communities at greatest risk improve access to timely clinical and laboratory services, including counseling, screening and treatment.

- CDC is working with our partners to implement effective health information campaigns, so that high-risk individuals are aware of the risk and know how to reduce it.

- Finally, our capacity to track or monitor syphilis has also been significantly stepped up. Today's study is a result of this effort.

This comprehensive approach . . . has begun to produce real progress toward our national goal of syphilis elimination and to have a profound impact on improving infant health.

I'll now turn the call over to Dr. George Counts, who will present our new data showing a significant reduction in syphilis among infants.

Syphilis Among Infants

George Counts: Syphilis among infants, known as congenital syphilis, is acquired when an infected pregnant woman transmits the infection to her fetus. Left untreated, up to 40% of congenital infections will result in infant death. Infected children who are not treated may suffer neurological impairment, seizures, deafness, or bone deformities.

Thankfully, if syphilis is detected in pregnant women, it can be treated with a single-dose of penicillin, an inexpensive, widely available antibiotic that is effective and safe for both mother and child.

Congenital syphilis data are reported to CDC from all 50 states and the District of Columbia. To evaluate progress in eliminating syphilis in the United States, CDC compared reported rates in 2000 with rates in 1997, the year before CDC syphilis elimination efforts began.

In 2000, 529 congenital syphilis cases were reported to CDC, representing approximately 13 of every 100,000 live births. *Overall, congenital syphilis rates dropped 51% since 1997.*

Cases in 2000 appeared in 155 counties, which represent only 5% of all counties in the United States. A regional breakdown of congenital syphilis shows that rates were highest in the South, with congenital syphilis occurring in approximately 19 of every 100,000 live births. Rates in other regions were significantly lower.

As in past years, minorities had the highest rates of congenital syphilis in 2000. African Americans had the highest rate—49.3 per 100,000 births—followed by Hispanics/Latinos at 22.6. The rate for whites was lowest, at 1.5.

Despite these continuing racial disparities, almost all racial groups experienced a significant drop in congenital syphilis rates. Rates declined 59.7% for African Americans and 58.3% for whites. Hispanics/Latinos experienced a smaller, but still significant decrease of 32.5%. The only racial group to experience a slight rise was American Indians/Alaska Natives, up by only one case.

Rates Among Women

When tracking congenital syphilis, it's also important to examine the rates of syphilis among women. Rates of congenital syphilis closely follow trends in infectious syphilis in women of reproductive age, as infants become infected from their mothers during pregnancy or delivery. In 2000, 2,219 infectious syphilis cases among women of childbearing age—age 15 to 44 years—were reported to CDC, a 38% drop from 3,590 cases in 1997, the year before the syphilis elimination campaign was begun.

A significant portion of the overall decline in syphilis among infants and women may be attributed to syphilis elimination programs initiated in recent years by CDC in collaboration with state and local partners. Many of these efforts have been targeted to the racial and ethnic minority communities that continue to report the highest rates of congenital syphilis, the majority of which are located in the South.

Despite these positive steps, many challenges remain. Racial and ethnic minorities continue to be disproportionately affected by congenital syphilis, as evidenced by the 33-to-1 ratio of African American to white cases. The high rates continue to be concentrated in the Southern states and a few northern and western urban areas. In some populations segments within these areas, limited access to comprehensive prenatal care— often as a result of poverty—may be a persistent barrier to the prevention of congenital syphilis.

Reported cases and rates of congenital syphilis in infants less than 1 year of age, 1963–2003

Year	Cases	Rate per 100,000 live births	Year	Cases	Rate per 100,000 live births
1963	367	9.2	1984	247	6.7
1964	336	8.7	1985	266	7.1
1965	335	8.9	1986	357	9.5
1966	333	8.8	1987	444	11.7
1967	156	4.1	1988	658	16.8
1968	274	7.3	1989	1,807	44.7
1969	264	7.0	1990	3,816	91.8
1970	323	8.6	1991	4,410	107.3
1971	422	11.9	1992	4,024	99.0
1972	360	11.0	1993	3,395	84.9
1973	295	9.4	1994	2,435	61.6
1974	250	7.9	1995	1,861	47.7
1975	169	5.3	1996	1,280	32.9
1976	160	5.1	1997	1,080	27.8
1977	134	4.0	1998	841	21.3
1978	104	3.0	1999	574	14.5
1979	123	3.5	2000	578	14.2
1980	107	3.0	2001	498	12.4
1981	160	4.4	2002	453	11.3
1982	159	4.3	2003	413	10.3
1983	158	4.3			

Note: The surveillance case definition for congenital syphilis changed in 1988. As of 1995, cases of congenital year of age are obtained using case reporting form CDC 73.126. For the period 1995 through 2003, yearly cases this table correspond to confirmed diagnoses of congenital syphilis among those known to be less than one year a result.

SOURCE: Center for Disease Control and Prevention, *STD Surveillance 2003*, Department of Health and Human Services, September 1994. www.cdc.gov.

Other challenges include the growing number of uninsured women, the limited expansion of prenatal care provided by Medicaid managed care and Child Health Insurance Programs, and the decreased funding of publicly funded clinics, emergency departments, and other safety net providers that serve poor, uninsured, racial and ethnic minority women and adolescents.

In order to effectively treat infected pregnant women, health care providers must regularly screen pregnant women. In a 1998 national survey, only 85% of obstetricians and gynecologists reported routinely screening their pregnant clients for syphilis.

Currently, CDC recommends that health care providers test all women for syphilis during the early stages of pregnancy. In areas where syphilis prevalence is high and for pregnant women at high risk for syphilis infection, CDC also recommends providers test their patients early during pregnancy and twice in the third trimester, including once at delivery. Because stillborn delivery can be due to syphilis, all women who deliver a stillborn infant after 20 weeks of gestation should also be tested for syphilis and treated if infected.

Syphilis screening should also be offered in emergency departments, jails, prisons and other settings that provide episodic care to pregnant women at high risk for syphilis. . . .

Let me make one point absolutely clear: elimination of congenital syphilis is a feasible goal because of the limited number of cases and its highly concentrated geographic distribution. The cornerstone of congenital syphilis prevention is early detection of maternal syphilis and treatment with safe and effective antibiotics. These simple actions could contribute to the complete elimination of syphilis among infants, and significantly improve infant health in the United States. If we fail to take advantage of this historic opportunity, the health of our families and our communities will continue to suffer.

A Tremendous Success

Judy Wasserheit: This study demonstrates that, through effective planning and coordination among national, state and local entities, both public and private, we have made remarkable strides in just a few short years.

Cutting rates of congenital syphilis in half in just three years is a tremendous success not simply because of the hundreds of babies who will enter the world healthy, but also because syphilis elimination activities appear to be improving prenatal care in many of our poorest, most vulnerable communities.

Through syphilis elimination activities, we cannot only save lives, but at the same time, save more than one billion dollars annually in direct and indirect health care costs associated with syphilis and its complications. Clearly, this goal must remain a public health priority.

Periodical Bibliography

The following articles have been selected to supplement the diverse views presented in this chapter.

Shaoni Bhattacharya "World AIDS Crisis Deepens and Spreads," *New Scientist*, July 2004.

Jim Brown "STD Epidemic a Result of People Not Paying Attention," *AFA Online*, October 25, 2002. http://headlines.agapepress.org.

Johannes L. Jacobse "Teen Sex Is Killing Our Kids," *OrthodoxyToday.org*, 2002. http://orthodoxytoday.org.

Ilsa L. Lottes "Sexual Health Policies in Other Industrialized Countries," *Journal of Sex Research*, February 2002.

Beatriz Pavon "Development Crisis: AIDS Slashes Life Expectancy in 23 African Countries," *UN Chronicle*, September/November 2004.

Elizabeth Terzakis "The Global AIDS Crisis," *International Socialist Review*, September 2002.

Stephen Vincent "'Multiple Epidemics' of Sexually Transmitted Diseases Devastate Millions," *National Catholic Register*, 2003.

Claudia Wallis "A Snapshot of Teen Sex," *Time*, February 17, 2004.

Paul S. Zeitz "Africans Need More than Our Sympathy," *Newsweek*, December 1, 2003.

**OPPOSING
VIEWPOINTS®
SERIES**

CHAPTER 2

How Should the Government Educate Youths About STDs?

Chapter Preface

The George W. Bush administration's increased funding of abstinence-only sex education programs has sparked new debate on the proper role of government in school-based sex education curricula. Currently, there are three federal programs dedicated to funding abstinence-only education: Section 510 of the Social Security Act, which was created as part of the 1996 welfare reform law; the Adolescent Family Life Act (AFLA); and Special Projects of Regional and National Significance (SPRANS). The central requirement for these programs is that they must have as their "exclusive purpose" the teaching of the benefits of abstinence. According to the American Civil Liberties Union, that means that "they may not advocate contraceptive use or teach contraceptive methods except to emphasize their failure rates." Essentially, this amounts to a gag order on any information on contraception and its use. Instead, the programs focus on the benefits of remaining sexually abstinent until marriage as a sure way to protect young people from sexually transmitted diseases (STDs). Some experts contend that abstinence-only programs are ineffective, while others claim they are the best way to reduce STDs.

Abstinence-only advocates claim that abstinence not only keeps young adults free from disease but also encourages discipline, morality, and robust mental health. "Instead of putting teens at risk of disease, premature parenthood and depression, abstinence empowers teenagers to practice self-control to avoid the detrimental consequences that accompany sexual activity," states Jessica Anderson, a writer for the conservative organization Concerned Women for America. Opponents of the abstinence-only approach to sex education argue that studies show that abstinence-only programs do not work. Critics also claim that these programs fail to provide accurate information that young people need to protect themselves from STDs and unwanted pregnancy. As Planned Parenthood Federation of America contends, studies show that "when they do become sexually active, teens who received abstinence-only education often fail to use condoms or other contraceptives." These commentators also claim that every reputable sex education organization in the United States, including prominent health organizations such as the American Medical Association, favor a comprehensive approach to the subject of sex education for young people.

With most conservatives favoring increased funding of abstinence-only programs, and most liberals supporting comprehensive sex education programs, this is a subject that will continue to be controversial for years to come.

| *"The government already spends far more promoting contraception than it does on abstinence education."*

The Government Should Promote Abstinence-Only Education

Melissa G. Pardue

According to Melissa G. Pardue in the following viewpoint, evidence shows that abstinence-only programs are effective in curtailing high-risk teen behaviors, particularly sexual activity. She argues that parents and students support the abstinence message, and she urges continued government funding for these programs. Pardue is a social welfare policy analyst for the Heritage Foundation, a conservative research and educational institute. She has published numerous papers and articles on poverty, marriage, abstinence education, and other social policy issues.

As you read, consider the following questions:

1. What were the results of the *Adolescent & Family Health*

Melissa G. Pardue, "More Evidence of the Effectiveness of Abstinence Education Programs," Webmemo #738, May 5, 2005, Copyright 2005 The Heritage Foundation. Reproduced by permission.

study published in 2005, according to Pardue?

2. How does Pardue describe the Best Friends program?

3. How much is spent on comprehensive sex education in contrast to abstinence only education, according to statistics cited by the author?

The harmful effects of early sexual activity are well documented. They include sexually transmitted diseases, teen pregnancy, and out-of-wedlock childbearing. As well, teen sexual activity is linked to emotional problems, such as depression, and increased risk of suicide. Abstinence education programs, which encourage teens to delay the onset of sexual activity, are effective in curbing such problems. Opponents of abstinence education, however, claim that abstinence programs don't work and that there has been [according to the Sexuality Information and Education Council of the United States (SIECUS),] "no scientific evidence that abstinence programs are effective." Research proves abstinence education opponents wrong once again.

A [2005] study by Dr. Robert Lerner published in the Institute for Youth Development's peer-reviewed journal *Adolescent & Family Health* bolsters the case for the effectiveness of abstinence programs in reducing teens' high-risk behaviors, including sexual activity, smoking, and alcohol and drug use. The study evaluates the effectiveness of the Best Friends abstinence education program and finds that students in it are significantly less likely than their peers to engage in any of these high-risk behaviors. This important research joins ten other evaluations that have also showed positive effects of abstinence programs.

Results of the Study

According to the study, released in April 2005, junior-high and middle-school-aged girls who participated in the Best Friends program, when compared to their peers who did not participate, were:

- Six-and-a-half times more likely to remain sexually abstinent;
- Nearly two times more likely to abstain from drinking alcohol;
- Eight times more likely to abstain from drug use; and
- Over two times more likely to refrain from smoking.

The Best Friends program began in 1987 and currently operates in more than 100 schools across the United States. Its curriculum consists of a character-building program for girls in the fifth or sixth grade, including at least 110 hours of instruction, mentoring, and group activities throughout the year. Discussion topics include friendship, love and dating, self-respect, decision-making, alcohol abuse, drug abuse, physical fitness and nutrition, and AIDS/STDs [sexually transmitted diseases]. The predominant theme of the curriculum is encouragement to abstain from high-risk behavior, including sexual activity. A companion program for boys, Best Men, began in 2000.

When girls who participate in the Best Friends program reach the 9th grade, they have the opportunity to enter the Diamond Girls Leadership program, which is designed to help girls maintain their commitment to abstinence. The Diamond Girls program offers opportunities to participate in a jazz choir or dance troupe, which help to foster discipline and social and presentation skills for the future.

A Highly Effective Program

According to the Lerner Study, the Best Friends program has been highly effective in reaching its goals. The study compared several years of data on girls from Washington, D.C., who participated in the Best Friends program with data on Washington, D.C., girls of the same age from the Centers for Disease Control's (CDC) Youth Risk Behavior Survey (YRBS).

The Benefits of Abstinence Education

Real abstinence education is essential to reducing out-of-wedlock childbearing, preventing sexually transmitted diseases, and improving emotional and physical well-being among the nation's youth. True abstinence education programs help young people to develop an understanding of commitment, fidelity, and intimacy that will serve them well as the foundations of healthy marital life in the future.

Robert E. Rector, The Heritage Foundation, April 8, 2002.
www.heritage.org.

Using multiple logistic regressions, which controlled for grade, age, race, and survey year, the study found a significant decrease in the incidence of high-risk behaviors among Best Friends girls as compared to YRBS girls. Specifically, girls who participated in the Best Friends program had:

- A 52 percent reduction in the likelihood that they would smoke;
- A 90 percent reduction in the likelihood that they would use drugs;
- A 60 percent reduction in the likelihood that they would drink alcohol; and
- An 80 percent reduction in the likelihood that they would have sex.

Other peer-reviewed studies have also found abstinence programs to be effective in reducing teen pregnancy and teen birthrates. An April 2003 study in *Adolescent & Family Health* found that increased abstinence among 15- to 19-year-old teens accounted for at least two-thirds (67%) of the drop in teen pregnancy rates. Increased abstinence also accounted for more than half (51%) of the decline in teen birthrates.

An August 2004 study in the *Journal of Adolescent Health* found similar results: 53 percent of the decline in teen pregnancy rates can be attributed to decreased sexual experience among teens aged 15–17 years old, while only 47 percent of the decline is attributed to increased use of contraception among teens.

Not surprisingly, parents overwhelmingly support the abstinence message. A December 2003 Zogby poll found that the overwhelming majority of parents—91 percent—want schools to teach that adolescents should be expected to abstain from sexual activity during high school years. Only 7 percent of parents believe that it is okay for teens in high school to engage in sexual intercourse as long as they use condoms, which is the predominant theme of "comprehensive" sex education.

Teens Embrace the Abstinence Message

Teens themselves welcome the abstinence message and appear to be heeding it. A December 2004 poll by the National Campaign to Prevent Teen Pregnancy found that a clear majority of adolescents—69 percent—agree that it is *not* okay for high school teens to engage in sexual intercourse. Data from the CDC confirms this, as the YRBS survey shows that the number of teens who have ever had sexual intercourse has fallen seven percent in the last 12 years, from 54 percent in 1991 to 46 percent in 2003.

Regrettably, groups like the Sexuality Information and Education Council of the United States (SIECUS) and Advocates for Youth would like to see abstinence programs eliminated and replaced with "comprehensive" sex education. These "comprehensive" programs are often misleadingly labeled "abstinence-plus" and falsely claim to be the middle ground between abstinence and safe sex education. This is not true. These programs are virtually all "plus" and almost no abstinence.

Analysis of "comprehensive" sex-ed programs reveals that these curricula contain little if any meaningful abstinence message. On average, these curricula devote about 4 percent of their content to abstinence. Out of 942 total pages of curriculum text reviewed from 9 different "comprehensive" sex-ed curricula, *not a single sentence* was found urging teens to abstain from sexual activity through high school. The overwhelming focus of these curricula (28 percent of the curriculum content) is devoted to promoting contraception among teens.

The government already spends far more promoting contraception than it does on abstinence education. In 2002 alone, federal and state governments spent $12 on safe sex and contraception promotion programs for every $1 spent on abstinence education. Yet some members of Congress would like to eliminate even this small amount of funding that encourages teen abstinence through programs like Best Friends.

Congressional opponents of abstinence education continue to attempt to introduce legislation that would abolish federal abstinence education assistance. For example, a proposal by Sen. Max Baucus (D-MT) would take federal funds that are devoted to teaching abstinence and turn them over to state public health bureaucracies to spend as they wish. Given the fact that such bureaucracies, through the encouragement of federal funding, have been wedded to the "safe sex" approach for decades and fiercely oppose teaching abstinence, such a proposal would effectively abolish federal abstinence education programs. These funds comprise nearly all the governmental support for teaching abstinence in U.S. schools.

Opponents of abstinence education will continue to try to eliminate it from America's schools. But they have got a tough pitch to make: Parents overwhelmingly support the abstinence message. Students want to hear it. The evidence of abstinence programs' effectiveness is increasing. And the evaluation of the Best Friends program provides yet one more argument in favor of abstinence education.

| "*'Abstinence-only' sex education programs ... are largely unproven [and] fail to provide young adults with the information they need to prevent pregnancy and STDs.*"

Abstinence-Only Education Is Ineffective

Patricia Miller

In the following viewpoint, journalist and reproductive rights expert Patricia Miller discusses what she sees as the failures of abstinence-only education, arguing that there have been studies that show that some abstinence-only education actually increases sexual activity among teens. Moreover, she maintains that abstinence-only programs promote a narrow moral view of sexuality, views that are promulgated by extremist organizations that oppose reproductive choice and women's equality.

As you read, consider the following questions:

1. When did the government begin funding abstinence-only sex education programs, according to Miller?

Patricia Miller from the Religious Coalition for Reproductive Choice Faith & Choices Newsletter, Spring 2004, pp. 8–10. Reproduced by permission.

2. How do abstinence-only programs distort facts about sex and contraception, in the author's opinion?

3. How does the author view evidence that abstinence-only sex education works?

A round the country, students are being told that condoms don't work to prevent AIDS, premarital sex leads to emotional instability and the inability to have a happy marriage, and people who have sex outside of marriage are immoral. And the government is paying for it. The [George W.] Bush administration has proposed doubling funding for "abstinence-only" sex education programs to $270 million, despite the fact that these programs are largely unproven, fail to provide young adults with the information they need to prevent pregnancy and STDs, and may violate the separation of church and state.

Abstinence-only programs rely on a fear-based curriculum to "scare" students away from all sexual activity while simultaneously promoting the belief that the only proper context for sex is marriage. For instance, students in McLennan County, Texas, are told that it's not uncommon for women to have genital warts "as large as two fists" hanging from their genitalia as a result of premarital sex and that using condoms "is like playing Russian roulette. There is a greater risk of condom failure than the bullet being in the chamber."

Students receiving "sex ed" from the FACTS program, which is used in the Portland, Oregon, area, are told "there is no such thing as 'safe' or 'safer' premarital sex. There are always risks associated with it, even dangerous, life-threatening ones." CLUE 2000, which was developed by Pure Love Alliance, a project of the Unification Church, says that "choosing to become sexually active can damage your ability to love, degrade your emotional self-worth and distort interpersonal relationships."

The Teen-Aid program tells young adults that "premarital sex, especially with more than one person, has been linked to the development of emotional illness." Among the laundry list of negative consequences of premarital sexual activity identified by [a program called] Facing Reality are: inability to concentrate on school, shotgun wedding, heartbreak, infertility, loneliness, cervical cancer, poverty, loss of self-esteem, suicide, substance abuse, loss of faith, difficulty with long-term commitments, loss of honesty, depression, and death.

As of 1999, one-third of all schools in the country were teaching abstinence exclusively, according to surveys by the Kaiser Family Foundation and the Alan Guttmacher Institute. And federal funding for abstinence-only education is set to double despite the fact that there is no scientific evidence that these programs work.

A History of Abstinence

Abstinence-only programs originated during the [Ronald] Reagan Administration with the Adolescent Family Life Act (AFLA), which was passed in 1981 to promote chastity among teens. Early AFLA programs frequently promoted specific religious values. The ACLU [American Civil Liberties Union] filed suit against AFLA programs in 1983 and, after a decade in court, in 1993 reached an out-of-court settlement that stipulated that AFLA programs would not include overt religious references and would be medically accurate and respect teens' self-determination in contraceptive choice.

In 1994, Rep. John Doolittle (R-CA) introduced a measure to restrict HIV prevention and sexuality education in school-based sex ed programs. This attempt was largely unsuccessful because of prohibitions on federal mandates on local curricula. Two years later, abstinence advocates launched a far more successful attempt to mandate abstinence-until-marriage education. Heritage Foundation policy analyst Robert Rector, a leading proponent of abstinence, worked with representatives from the Family Research Council, the Christian Coalition, and other conservative groups to draft a measure that was included in the 1996 welfare reform bill. The measure provided a new entitlement program to encourage states to promote abstinence and funded it at $50 million a year over five years.

Funding for abstinence-only has increased steadily since 1996. Total spending on abstinence-only education, including the welfare-reform and AFLA programs, was $80 million in 2001, and increased to $100 million in 2002 and $120 million in 2003. Bush . . . proposed spending $270 million in 2005. . . . "What Congress has to realize is that, by denying youth critical information about contraception and prevention in the era of AIDS, they are placing the health and lives of young people in jeopardy," said James Wagoner, president of Advocates for Youth.

The Whole Story

States that accept the abstinence-only money are required to adhere to a strict, eight-point definition of abstinence education, which includes the following principles:

- "Sexual activity outside of marriage is likely to have harmful psychological and physical effects."
- "Abstinence from sexual activity is the only certain way to avoid out-of-wedlock pregnancy, sexually transmitted diseases, and other associated health problems."
- "A mutually faithful monogamous relationship in the context of marriage is the expected standard of human sexual activity."

Advocates of comprehensive sex education—which educates teens about the benefits of delaying sexual activity but also includes information about contraceptives and STD prevention—point to a number of problems with the abstinence approach. According to a report by the Sexuality Information and Education Council of the United States (SIECUS), abstinence-only programs deny young adults the information they need to make "informed, responsible decisions about their sexuality."

These programs deny the reality that most teenagers engage in increasingly intimate sexual behaviors as they age and that, according to the Centers for Disease Control and Prevention (CDC), 50 percent of high school students have had sexual intercourse. In addition, the requirement that abstinence programs discuss abstinence as the only sure way to avoid STDs "clearly prevents funded programs from discussing the effectiveness of condoms and contraception in preventing unintended pregnancy and disease transmission" and discourages the use of condoms.

Abstinence-only programs also routinely suggest that condoms and other contraceptives are unreliable. The Choosing the Best program tells teens that condoms fail more than 25 percent of the time and that condoms are extremely difficult to use, requiring more than 10 steps, including the bizarre statement that the final, post-intercourse step to condom use is cleaning the genital area with "rubbing alcohol or dilute solutions of Lysol."

According to SIECUS, abstinence-only programs prominently discuss the most extreme consequences of untreated STDs and fail to discuss routine STD prevention and screening, which leaves sexually active teens at risk. Sexuality educator Debbie Roffman, author of *Sex and Sensibility: The Thinking Parent's Guide to Talking Sense About Sex*, says that efforts to scare teens away from sex with horror stories can backfire because it erodes their sense of control. "You want kids to be appropriately concerned, but you also want to leave them feeling in control. Tell them the truth, but tell them the good news is that these are preventable diseases—there are many things you can do to prevent them," she said.

The programs' emphasis on abstinence until marriage as the "expected standard" also flies in the face of the fact that the vast majority of men and women are not virgins when

Abstinence Education Is Dangerous

While abstinence is certainly an effective method of preventing HIV/AIDS as well as other sexually-transmitted diseases or unwanted pregnancy, abstinence-only education is impractical and downright dangerous when implemented to the exclusion of a broader and more inclusive approach to sex education.

Mary Shaw, Online Journal, *January 18, 2005.*

they marry. They also assume that all people desire to enter into a "mutually faithful monogamous relationship in the context of marriage," disregarding people who choose not to marry and gays and lesbians who are legally barred from marrying. The programs also promote the idea that sexual activity outside of marriage is harmful, when there is no evidence to prove this is true and most people engage in sexual activity prior [to] or outside of marriage with no negative consequences.

The programs also attempt to stigmatize premarital sex as immoral and shameful. The Nevada State Health Division was forced to suspend public service announcements for its abstinence-only program after they generated controversy. The ads proclaimed that teenage girls often feel "dirty and cheap" when they break up with boyfriends they have had sex with, that condoms don't protect against some STDs, and that sexually active teens are more likely to commit suicide.

The Evidence

In addition to delivering messages that may harm teens, abstinence-only programs are largely unproven as to their effectiveness in meeting basic public health goals such as preventing teen pregnancy and delaying sexual intercourse. A 2001 report by then-Surgeon General David Satcher said that there was no evidence that abstinence-only programs work and said sex ed programs should provide information on contraceptives and safe sex practices. The report called for "access to education about sexual health and responsible sexual behavior that is thorough, wide-ranging, [and] begins early."

There is evidence that abstinence programs may be damaging to teens. A study [that came] out in February [2004] found that a five-year, federally funded abstinence-only program in Minnesota called "Minnesota Education Now and Babies Later" actually increased sexual activity among teens and increased expectations among teens that they would be sexually active.

There has been an overall 28% decline in teen pregnancy over the past decade. While most sexual health experts attribute the decline to an increase in contraceptive use and a decrease in sexual activity due to better education, particularly about AIDS, abstinence advocates say the decline shows the effectiveness of abstinence education. "As abstinence education has spread from a few classrooms in the 1980s to thousands of schools across the country today, the message is getting through. Teens are making decisions for virginity, and the results are clear," said Leslee Unruh, president of the Abstinence Clearinghouse, which serves as a resource for abstinence-only programs.

The Heritage Foundation released a review of 10 "promising" abstinence-only programs, but none of the studies were peer-reviewed and most of the programs were small and had been operating for only a short time. The study did find that teens who took "virginity pledges" delayed sexual activity for 18 months longer than those who did not, but in a finding that seems to support the worst fears of comprehensive sexuality advocates, teens who took the pledge were more likely not to use contraceptives once they did become sexually active.

A review of comprehensive sex ed programs sponsored by the National Campaign to Prevent Teen Pregnancy found that these types of programs do not promote sexual activity among teens, as abstinence advocates charge. The review also found no evidence that abstinence-only programs were effective.

The public supports comprehensive sex education. A recent poll found that only 15% of Americans believe that schools should teach abstinence-only and withhold information on contraceptives. The vast majority said that teens should be taught a more comprehensive approach; either one that stresses abstinence as the best approach but provides information on contraceptives (46%) or primarily focuses on teaching teens how to make responsible decisions about sex (36%).

Whose Morality Is It, Anyway?

In addition to being unproven programs that deprive sexually developing teens of the information they need to make wise decisions, abstinence-only programs promote a narrow moral view about the role of sexuality in human relationship supported by extremist organizations that oppose reproductive choice and women's equality. According to Cornell University Law Professor Gary Simson, abstinence-only programs may violate the First Amendment because they "are rooted in the purpose of endorsing the view of sex urged by, and identified with, the Christian Coalition and its allies in the 'religious right.'" Simon says that programs like Sex Respect are designed to "give effect to the conservative Christian view that both premarital sex and homosexual conduct are sinful and therefore to be avoided."

A federal judge found in 2002 that an abstinence-only program widely used in Louisiana schools improperly advanced religion and promoted religious messages. Money in the program was used to hold prayer rallies outside of abortion clinics and [to] perform "Christ-centered" skits with abstinence messages. One program used the virgin birth to emphasize God's desire for "sexual purity." Under an agreement reached with the ACLU, the state will monitor future program content for religious references.

People of faith overwhelmingly support providing young adults with the accurate information about sexuality that they need to make responsible choices. A national poll of 900 voters commissioned by the Religious Coalition for Reproductive Choice found that Americans of all faiths want responsible sexuality education taught in schools, including 73% of Catholics and 67% of Christian fundamentalists. Religious support for sexuality education is long-standing. In 1968, influential Protestant, Catholic, and Jewish organizations released a joint statement calling for each community to provide "resources, leadership and opportunities as appropriate" for sexuality education in light of their religious tradition.

The American Baptist Church, the Episcopal Church, the Presbyterian Church (USA), the Unitarian Universalist Association, the United Church of Christ, the United Methodist Church, and Reform and Conservative Judaism have passed resolutions affirming the need for sexuality education within their own faiths and the public schools. The Religious Coalition has several resources to help provide faith-based comprehensive sexuality education. In addition, the [coalition president] Rev. Carlton Veazey is serving on Dr. David Satcher's National Advisory Council on Sexual Health, which is working to promote sexual health and responsible sexual behavior.

But conservatives are busy as well. In addition to the doubling of funds for abstinence education . . . , the next frontier for abstinence education is adults. Robert Rector envisions promoting the gospel of abstinence to young adults in their 20s as well as teens—a move that dovetails with Bush administration plans to devote $1.5 billion to promote marriage, especially among low-income men and women, to reduce out-of-wedlock births. But many public health experts argue that there is a better way to reduce illegitimacy than coercing poor women into marriage—comprehensive education about sex and family planning options.

> "Averting the dollars misspent [by government] on abstinence-only education to start-up a comprehensive sex-ed program would be the responsible choice."

The Government Should Fund Comprehensive Sex Education Programs

Louise Melling

In the following viewpoint, Louise Melling maintains that comprehensive sex education that teaches youths to have sex responsibly is the best way to decrease rates of sexually transmitted diseases and teen pregnancy. She notes the growing body of evidence that suggests that abstinence-only programs do not work and in fact mislead teens into indulging in high-risk sexual behaviors. Melling is the director of the American Civil Liberties Union's Reproductive Freedom Project.

As you read, consider the following questions:

1. By how much does Melling say the federal government increased funding for abstinence-only education in 2006?

2. What is the Responsible Education About Life (REAL) Act, according to Melling?

3. Why does the author believe that comprehensive sex education programs are more effective than abstinence-only programs in the fight against STDs and teen pregnancies?

Censorship. Misinformation. Indoctrination. Parents don't associate these words with their children's education, and taxpayers don't expect such practices to be funded by millions of federal dollars. Yet when President [George W.] Bush proposed a $39 million increase in federal funding for abstinence-only-until-marriage sex education in his 2006 budget, he asked Congress to do just that. If the president gets what he asked for, the federal government will throw nearly $206 million in fiscal year [2006] into programs that a growing body of evidence shows are ineffective at best, and dangerous at worst.

Truth. Accuracy. Responsibility. The Responsible Education About Life (REAL) Act, introduced . . . by lawmakers in both houses of Congress, is the antidote to unproven, misleading, and harmful abstinence-only sex education. Federal abstinence-only programs must focus exclusively on abstinence and are often prohibited from discussing contraceptives except to emphasize their failure rates. REAL programs would teach that abstinence is the only sure way to avoid pregnancy or sexually transmitted infections, but they would also include information about how to use contraceptives to prevent pregnancy and infection. In addition, REAL would require funded programs to provide age-appropriate and medically accurate information and to refrain from using taxpayer dollars to preach religion, a constitutional safeguard that many abstinence-only programs fail to provide.

In the current political climate, the chance that this commonsense legislation becomes law: 0. The chance that abstinence-only programs get a substantial increase: 100.

In a budget that includes the deepest cuts to domestic spending in two decades, including huge reductions to health care programs for the poor, food stamps, and research on chronic diseases, what's responsible about increasing funding for ineffective abstinence-only education?

According to the most recent statistics, 822,000 15–19 year old women got pregnant in 2000, and each year, approximately 9.1 million 15–24 year olds are infected with sexually transmitted infections, including one-half of all new HIV infections. A growing body of evidence shows that most abstinence-only programs do not help teens delay having sex, and some show evidence of increasing risk-taking behaviors among sexually active teens.

Comprehensive Programs Work

On the other hand, evidence shows that comprehensive programs that provide information about abstinence and effective use of contraception can help delay the start of sexual activity and increase condom use among sexually active teens. Yet there is currently no federal program dedicated to comprehensive sex education. Averting the dollars misspent on abstinence-only education to start-up a comprehensive sex-ed program would be the responsible choice.

Leaving the effectiveness question aside, what about truth and accuracy? A recent review of federally funded abstinence-only curricula prepared by Representative Henry A. Waxman (D, CA) found that more than two-thirds of the programs reviewed distort information about contraceptives, misrepresent the risks of abortion, blur religion and science, promote gender stereotypes, and contain basic scientific errors. Backed

Arguments for Comprehensive Sex Education

Comprehensive sex education proponents argue that "[b]y denying teens the full range of information regarding human sexuality, abstinence-only education fails to provide young people with the information they need to protect their health and well-being." And surveys of young people conducted by the Kaiser Family Foundation found that "students who have sex education—regardless of the curriculum—know more and feel better prepared to handle different situations and decisions than those who have not."

Chris Collins, Priya Alagiri, and Todd Summers,
AIDS Research Institute, University of California–San Francisco,
March 2002.

by no credible evidence, one curriculum wrongly asserts that 5 percent to 10 percent of women who have abortions will become sterile. Another incorrectly suggests that HIV can be contracted through exposure to sweat and tears. Yet, when lawmakers attempted to add a medical accuracy requirement to one stream of federal abstinence-only funding, the effort fell on deaf ears.

The American Civil Liberties Union [ACLU] knows all too well about the blurring of the line between religion and science in abstinence-only curricula. In 2002, the ACLU successfully sued the Louisiana Governor's Program on Abstinence for using federal dollars to support religious activities, including Christ-centered theater skits, religious youth revivals, and gospel radio shows. The governor's program agreed to settle the case and was later ordered by the court to closely monitor the activities of all funded programs and to stop using public money to "convey religious messages or otherwise advance religion in any way." Despite this agreement, problems persist. [In January 2005], the ACLU asked a federal court to hold the governor's program in contempt for using their state-sponsored abstinence-only website to proselytize. . . .

Defending his budget, Bush rightly asserted, "A taxpayer dollar ought to be spent wisely or not spent at all." In continuing to fund abstinence-only education and in further asking for an increase in spending, the Bush administration has shown that it is not interested in spending wisely or responsibly. When it comes to protecting America's youth, REAL is clearly the wise choice. Unfortunately, under Bush's spendthrift approach to sex education, it is precisely America's youth that will continue to pay too high a price for government irresponsibility.

"*Abstinence programs work for the simple reason that kids can keep their hormones in check.*"

The Government Should Not Fund Comprehensive Sex Education Programs

Joel Mowbray

In the following viewpoint, writer Joel Mowbray contrasts abstinence-only and abstinence-plus sex education programs, claiming that the latter are actually comprehensive sex education programs. Mowbray asserts that federal funding for sex education programs should go only to those that feature an abstinence-only curriculum. He questions some of the exercises included in the abstinence-plus classes—such as finding sensual alternatives to sexual activity—and suggests that they encourage promiscuity among adolescents. Moreover, he argues, studies show that abstinence-only programs work to delay sexual activity and decrease rates of sexually transmitted diseases and teen pregnancy. Mowbray is a syndicated columnist and the author of Dangerous Diplomacy.

Joel Mowbray, "Abstinence Works," *National Review Online*, April 12, 2002. Copyright 2002 by National Review, Inc., 215 Lexington Avenue, New York, NY 10016. Reproduced by permission.

As you read, consider the following questions:

1. According to Mowbray, what are the differences between abstinence-only and abstinence-plus sex education programs?

2. Why does the author oppose abstinence-plus sex education programs?

3. What evidence does the author present that abstinence-only programs work?

A battle is brewing on Capitol Hill between two rather similar-sounding concepts, abstinence-only and abstinence-plus [sex] education, but the differences couldn't be greater—or more shocking. Despite the "abstinence" in the name, parents would be appalled to see the sexually explicit material peddled to kids in abstinence-plus programs.

Under current federal law, there are two basic approaches, abstinence-only and comprehensive sex education, and the latter receives far more cash. This issue is much larger than just money going to schools, as funds go to outside groups as part of a whole host of federal programs, including welfare and education block grants.

President George W. Bush's campaign pledge, on which he is trying to make good, would bring abstinence, which focuses heavily on marriage and the value of waiting, and traditional sex ed, which emphasizes safe sex when "hooking up," into funding parity. But there's a big hurdle to clear in the interim. Leftist groups like Planned Parenthood are scheming to change the federal government's insistence for abstinence-only to the mislabeled abstinence-plus programs.

To get a glimpse of the practical implications of this debate, look no further than a [2002] report released by Physicians Consortium, a socially conservative group representing 2,000 doctors. The Centers for Disease Control (CDC) already monitors state- and locally funded sex-ed courses and

Dangerous Teachings

What is really best for . . . youth? Below is just a sample of the content from . . . so-called "comprehensive" sex education programs. . . .

- **Be Proud! Be Responsible** (for adolescents)— "Go to the store together. Buy lots of different brands and colors [of condoms]. Plan a special day when you can experiment. Just talking about how you'll use all of those condoms can be a turn on."
- **Focus on Kids** (ages 9–15)—Assigns teens to create a list of ways to be close to a person without having intercourse, including, "body massage, bathing together, masturbation, sensuous feeding, fantasizing, watching erotic movies, reading erotic books and magazines."

Illinois Family Institute, "Grape Jelly Is for Toast, not Condom Lessons in School," March 23, 2005. www.illinoisfamily.org.

promotes ones it finds particularly effective to middle and high schools in an official initiative called "Programs That Work."

Programs That Work?

In one exercise, students are encouraged to pursue various alternatives to sexual intercourse. So far, so good. But the recommended activities? Body massage, bathing together, "sensuous feeding," joint masturbation, and watching "erotic movies." Of course, when teens engage in these not-quite PG-13 activities, they'll no doubt be satisfied and exclaim, "Wow—thank goodness I have no need to have sex now!"

Taking the prize for sheer absurdity, however, is a priceless exercise called the "Condom Race." Students are divided into two teams, and every child is handed a condom. Forming two lines, each student has to put condoms on and remove them from his or her team's designated "cucumber or dildo." The team that finishes first, wins.

Perhaps the most disturbing element of both these programs is the target demographic: 9 to 15 year olds. Rather than condemning these courses as purveyors of promiscuity to young children, the CDC lauds them as model examples for others to emulate.

If abstinence-plus becomes the law of the land at the federal level, outlandish and offensive "abstinence" programs would replace abstinence-only ones that have logged significant success in recent years.

Given that three million teenagers contract sexually transmitted diseases *every year*, reducing sexual activity—not just making it "safer" —is imperative. A report from the Heritage Foundation's Robert Rector compiles ten separate scientific evaluations of abstinence programs throughout the country, and each course analyzed has made significant strides in keeping kids out of compromising positions.

Abstinence-Only Education Produces Results

Promoting abstinence works both in the classroom and through a public-relations campaign. Abstinence by Choice, which operates in 20 schools in and around Little Rock, Arkansas, has had a measurable impact on the lives of the 4,000 7th–9th graders it reaches each year. Sexual-activity rates among boys plunged 30 percent, and the rate for girls plummeted 40 percent.

Not Me, Not Now is a community-wide campaign that targets 9 to 14 year olds in Monroe County, New York, which includes the city of Rochester. The abstinence program spreads its message through billboards, paid TV and radio ads, an interactive website, posters in schools, educational materials for parents, and sessions in school and community settings. Not Me, Not Now is effective, achieving 95-percent awareness among its target demographic, slashing the sexual-activity rate of 15 year olds in the county by over 30 percent, and reducing the pregnancy rate among 15 to 17 year olds by nearly 25 percent.

Sometimes something as simple as a commitment to abstinence can yield results. Rector's analysis of several comprehensive studies found that virginity-pledge programs show progress. In one study, the level of sexual activity among teens who had taken a formal pledge of virginity was *one-fourth* that of their peers who had taken no such pledge. Obviously students who would be willing to take such a pledge in the first place have a natural inclination toward chaste behavior, but a 75 percent reduction is awfully compelling.

Abstinence programs work for the simple reason that kids can keep their hormones in check. Though they may seem like it at times, teenagers don't lack human willpower. Kids can, and often do, take a message of responsibility to heart.

When the slugfest starts over the type of abstinence education funded at the federal level, don't be fooled by the term "abstinence-plus." More than half of all federal dollars already go to programs that push comprehensive sex ed, including all sorts of information about safe sex and condoms. Given that funding disparity, money devoted to abstinence should actually promote abstinence. It's that simple.

> "*[African American] children need information on how to protect themselves when they are sexually active, as well as support in delaying that sexual activity until they are capable of handling it.*"

The Government Should Spend More on Sex Education in the African American Community

Kai Wright

In the following viewpoint, Kai Wright presents poll results indicating African American parents prefer comprehensive sex education programs over abstinence-only education. Youths need to be taught how to have sex responsibly, the parents believe. Wright concludes that the epidemic of AIDS in the African American community is too important to be left to right-wing politicians trying to make a moral argument. Wright is a journalist whose articles on the politics of race and sex appear in magazines such as Out, Poz, *and the* Progressive.

As you read, consider the following questions:

1. What percentage of African American parents does Wright say believe their children should be taught comprehensive sex education?

2. Why does the author believe that abstinence-only programs do not work?

3. Why does the author favor comprehensive sex education programs over abstinence-only sex education programs in the African American community?

Current research is making at least one thing clear: the success that we have seen in reducing sexual risk behavior among youth is being jeopardized by Washington's increasing embrace of "abstinence-only" sex education.

Throughout the last decade, sexual health experts both inside and out of government agreed that what is known as "comprehensive" sex education made the most sense for our schools. Comprehensive sex ed stresses the value of delaying sexual activity until adulthood, but also gives youth all of the information they need to prevent diseases and pregnancies should they decide to have sex. As the CDC [Centers for Disease Control and Prevention] states on its website, "Research has clearly shown that the most effective programs are comprehensive ones that include a focus on delaying sexual behavior *and* provide information on how sexually active young people can protect themselves. Evidence of prevention success can be seen in trends from the Youth Risk Behavior Survey conducted over an 8-year period, which show both a decline in sexual risk behaviors and an increase in condom use among sexually active youth." (Italics in original.)

More-targeted studies have also shown that comprehensive sex education programs in schools reduce risk-taking in sexually active youth without increasing the likelihood that those who are not having sex will begin to do so. Indeed, one study in Massachusetts found that students attending schools where condoms are made available are both less likely to be sexually active and twice as likely to use condoms when they eventually do have sex. This is the sort of research that prompted then-Surgeon General David Satcher to state in his 2001 "Call to Action" on sexual health, "Few would disagree that parents should be the primary sexuality educators of their children or that sexual abstinence until engaged in a committed and mutually monogamous relationship is an important component in any sexuality education program. It does seem clear, however, that providing sexuality education in the schools is a useful mechanism to ensure that this nation's youth have a basic understanding of sexuality. Traditionally, schools have had a role in ensuring equity of access to information that is perhaps greater than most other institutions. In addition, given that one-half of adolescents in the United States are already sexually active—and at risk of unintended pregnancy and STD/HIV infection—it also seems clear that adolescents need accurate information about contraceptive methods so that they can reduce those risks."

African American parents agree with Dr. Satcher. A CDC survey of 680 Black parents found that 97 percent believe they should be teaching their pre-teen kids about sex-related topics and 88 percent don't think that doing so will encourage their kids to have sex.

The Rise of Abstinence-Only Sex Ed

But in recent years, Congress and the [George W.] Bush administration have broken away from the consensus on comprehensive sex education. In 1996, conservative lawmakers slipped a program to fund abstinence-only sex education programs into a massive bill reshaping the welfare system. The measure set aside $250 million over the following five years for state-run abstinence programs, and required states to put up matching funds if they took the federal money. The law stipulates that abstinence-only programs meet a strict set of guidelines, which include teaching that "sexual activity outside of marriage is likely to have harmful psychological and physical effects."

Abstinence-only programs believe talking about safer sex techniques such as condom use and masturbation encourages sexual behavior, and they thus discuss condoms only to point out their potential deficiencies. To date, there exists no federal funding set-aside for comprehensive sex education. The funding for abstinence-only education in the welfare bill was not the first time conservative legislators delineated money for these programs. Nevertheless, this latest round was nominally to fund a pilot program, meant to test the efficacy of abstinence-only education. But the only measure by which the programs were to be graded was whether they increased the number of kids who said they want to be abstinent. The programs were not held accountable for actual sexual behavior, and the funding has since been renewed.

No Evidence that Abstinence Works

It's a good thing for those programs that they haven't had to stand up to scrutiny. To date, there exists no research showing abstinence-only programs delay the onset of sexual activity. There is, however, a mounting pile of research suggesting that they not only fail to slow sexual activity, but may also put kids at greater risk for disease. A popular aspect of abstinence programs is the "virginity pledge" that students take, in which they vow to either remain a virgin or to re-embrace abstinence if they have already had sex. One large-scale, national study found virginity pledges can in fact delay the onset of sexual activity, but only when they are built around a relatively small group of youth reinforcing one another as part of a counter-cultural identity. The participating youth must build what the authors call a "moral community" and define themselves against the larger social environment they are navigating; for the pledge to have effect, they must be virgins in a sea of

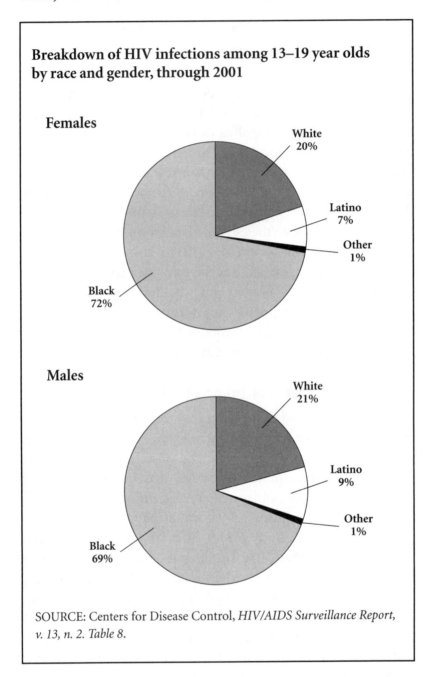

Breakdown of HIV infections among 13–19 year olds by race and gender, through 2001

Females

White 20%

Latino 7%

Other 1%

Black 72%

Males

White 21%

Latino 9%

Other 1%

Black 69%

SOURCE: Centers for Disease Control, *HIV/AIDS Surveillance Report, v. 13, n. 2. Table 8.*

whores. But the pledges still delayed sexual intercourse for an average of just 18 months. And when the youth who had taken the pledge eventually had sex, they were less likely to use contraception than those who had not.

But more troubling data comes from state-level evaluations of the abstinence programs that were launched with the funding provided under the welfare reform law. In the first five years of the initiative, every state but California accepted the federal money and launched an abstinence program. (California balked at the money because it had just completed its own pilot on abstinence-only education and had found that the programs did not work.) All told, around $500 million in federal and state money was funneled into these programs between 1998 and 2003. In 2004, Advocates for Youth, a progressive organization that promotes youth sexual health, culled information from 10 of the state evaluations that were publicly available, along with California's evaluation of its earlier pilot. Despite stipulations in the law that all the states review their programs' efficacy, Congress renewed the funding without having seen many state evaluations.

The Advocates for Youth review found that, of the 10 program evaluations available, three showed the programs having no impact on sexual behavior at all and two actually showed an *increase* in sexual activity among participating youth. Even looking just at the participants' intentions, only four state programs saw a favorable impact in their students' intentions to abstain from sex.

The Waxman Study

Meanwhile, California Congressmember Henry Waxman ordered a study of the abstinence-only programs funded through new Bush Administration initiatives, which ... total $104 million for fiscal year 2005. Waxman's study found that 80 percent of the curricula used by the programs that the U.S. Department of Health and Human Services (HHS) funds contain information that is "false, misleading or distorted."

Those curricula were used by more than two-thirds of the programs that HHS funded in 2003. Much of the information provided by these federally-funded programs was not only false, but spectacularly so. One curriculum taught that as much as 10 percent of abortions cause sterility. Another teaches that HIV can be transmitted through sweat and tears. Another asserted that condoms failed to prevent HIV almost a third of the time they are used. Moreover, they not only blurred the lines between religion and science, they promoted negative gender stereotypes. One curriculum taught that, as a rule, women are seeking "financial support" in their relationships while men seek "admiration." Another asserted, "Women gauge their happiness and judge their success on their relationships. Men's happiness and success hinge on their accomplishments."

All told, the federal government [spent] $167 million on these sorts of sex education programs in fiscal year 2005. The White House had proposed spending $270 million. Since the Bush Administration has taken office, funding for abstinence-only education has more than doubled, largely driven by funding for the HHS programs described in Rep. Waxman's report.

What Rep. Waxman's report implies is that, ultimately, these programs are less interested in helping young people remain sexually healthy than they are in fighting the culture wars. For African Americans, far too much is at stake to allow our children to be caught in the crossfire of the national fight over sexual morality. Our children need information on how to protect themselves when they are sexually active, as well as support in delaying that sexual activity until they are capable of handling it. Science shows that, when they are given useful and valid information, youth are making increasingly healthy choices. Research shows that African American parents overwhelmingly agree. And, yet, our federal government has launched an effort to silence these vital conversations in our schools by tying federal support to abstinence-only messages. African Americans must stand up and fight this backdoor censorship.

| *"It is time that everyone, particularly African Americans, take responsibility for [the AIDS epidemic's] longevity."*

Greater Individual Responsibility Can Reduce STDs in the African American Community

Phill Wilson

In the following viewpoint, Phill Wilson claims that AIDS is ravaging the African American community. He encourages every African American to get tested; those who are HIV-positive should hold themselves accountable for their sexual practices as well as their own health. Wilson is a writer and the director of the Los Angeles–based Black AIDS Institute, an African American HIV/AIDS center.

As you read, consider the following questions:

1. What percentage of Americans living with AIDS are African Americans, according to Wilson?

2. Why is June 12, 2005, a milestone, in the author's opinion?

3. Why does the author believe that the African American community needs to be more accountable in the fight against HIV/AIDS?

On Monday, June 12, [2005,] the U.S. Centers for Disease Control and Prevention [CDC] announced that African Americans represent about half of all people living with HIV in the country. *Half!* We're only 13 percent of the population. We already knew three quarters of new female infections are among African American women, who are getting HIV largely through sex.

It gets worse. CDC also revealed a study—the first in a series that the agency hopes will give us unprecedented specifics about the number and nature of HIV infections in America—suggesting that half of all Black homosexual and bisexual men are already positive.

Meanwhile, improvements we once saw among youth are reversing. After declining by 30 percent throughout the 1990s, the number of new HIV infections among young men of all races shot up 41 percent between 1999 and 2003.

For more than two decades now, AIDS activists have rightly asserted that this is not just any other disease. It's a virus that preys upon the most marginalized in our society. As a result, infection continues to carry great deals of stigma. It is, after all, a sexually transmitted disease, and one that is most likely to affect those who are having anal sex or using drugs.

A New Era

But on June 12 [2005] we entered a new era. We can no longer afford to trifle with the politics of America's culture wars, whether they come from the left or the right. It is time that everyone, particularly African Americans, take responsibility

Individual Accountability Is Crucial

Accountability is most important on an individual level. We are each responsible for keeping ourselves healthy, for keeping our communities engaged, and for keeping our leaders vigilant. We may not know much about this [AIDS] epidemic, but we know this: If we all demand accountability of ourselves, we can make a change.

BlackAIDS.org,
"Better Questions, Better Answers," June 15, 2005.
http://306.196.5.81/prod.blackaids.org.

for this monster's longevity. Individuals, community organizers and policymakers must all begin to hold themselves accountable.

Be Accountable

As individuals, two things are clear. First, every African American who does not know whether he or she is HIV positive or negative has the ability to find out. Free, confidential testing is available in every part of this country. Go find out your status. Be accountable.

Second, every one of us who know we are HIV positive have the ability to stop the virus' spread, to not allow ourselves to be a link in the insidious chain. Similarly, everyone who is negative has the ability to stay that way, by taking responsibility for your own health. Be accountable.

The community organizers who have rightly taken the lead in HIV prevention to date must also accept the new reality. We can no longer afford to spend our limited resources on initiatives that just make us all feel good. Our prevention campaigns must be accountable to scientific standards; if we can't show they work then we need to put our resources into what does.

But accountability doesn't stop there. Individuals and communities need support in their efforts, and government—at both local and national levels—must be a far more responsible partner than it has been so far.

The White House is pushing a $4 million cut to the CDC's HIV and STD prevention budget for the coming fiscal year. That comes after two previous years of cutting an already measly budget. This, as Washington prepares to hand out yet another round of billions of dollars in tax cuts to the wealthy.

Politics

Meanwhile, religion and politics rather than science continue to guide the federal government's role in prevention. An early 1990s regulation prevents the CDC from funding any prevention campaign deemed to "promote" sex. Rightwing legislators have repeatedly used the bizarre rule to browbeat any community group trying to develop innovative interventions that speak honestly about what is, I repeat, a sexually transmitted disease.

Washington has also begun shoving aside the school-based, comprehensive sex education that has proven effective, in favor of unproven abstinence-only curricula—which forbids any discussion of how to use a condom or avoid STDs once you are sexually active. Politicians must get out of the way and let science rule the day, and we must hold them accountable when they don't.

We have dithered too long. The awful data the CDC revealed on June 12 is unassailable proof of that fact. So what now? It's time for all of us to take responsibility for stopping this slaughter.

Periodical Bibliography

The following articles have been selected to supplement the diverse views presented in this chapter.

Ceci Connolly "Some Abstinence Programs Mislead Teens, Report Says," *Washington Post*, December 2, 2004.

Charles Dervarics "Conspiracy Beliefs May Be Hindering HIV Prevention Among African Americans," Population Reference Bureau, March 2005. www .prb.org.

LeeChe Leong "Virulent Virginity: 'Abstinence-Only' Sex Education Programs Are Putting Youth at Risk," *ColorLines*, Winter 2004.

George Monbiot "Joy of Sex Education," *Guardian* (Manchester, UK), May 11, 2004.

Kate Petre "The Sexual Mis-education of the American Teen," *Los Angeles City Beat*, January 13, 2005. www.lacitybeat.com.

Robert Rector "Aborting Abstinence," *National Review Online*, April 29, 2005. http://www.nationalreview.com.

Sarah Sparks "Abstinence Programs May Give Attitude Adjustment," *Education Daily*, June 16, 2005.

Karen Springen "Beyond the Birds and Bees," *Newsweek*, April 25, 2005.

Dana Wilkie "Debate Grows over the Teaching of Abstinence," *San Diego Union-Tribune*, June 16, 2005.

CHAPTER 3

How Can Individuals Reduce the Spread of Sexually Transmitted Diseases?

Chapter Preface

Personal responsibility has always been a controversial topic when it comes to discussions of sex and the spread of sexually transmitted diseases (STDs). One way to encourage personal responsibility in teens is to ask them to take virginity pledges. Many experts claim that abstinence is the only completely effective way to protect individuals from STDs and unwanted pregnancy. Other commentators assert that abstinence is unrealistic and ultimately fails to protect young people.

For those who stress the issue of personal responsibility for young people, virginity pledges (also called abstinence pledges) have become a popular method of reinforcing an abstinence approach to sex education. Usually religion based, abstinence pledges require pledgers to remain sexually abstinent until they get married. A June 2005 study by the Heritage Foundation, a conservative think tank, finds that teens who take such pledges are twelve times more likely to remain virgins until marriage, one-third less likely to become pregnant during high school, and 40 percent less likely to have a baby outside of marriage. The study also finds that pledgers have fewer sexual partners and delay sexual activity by three years or so. According to Robert Rector and Kirk A. Johnson, authors of the Heritage study, "Overall, virginity pledge programs have a strong record of success. They are among the few institutions in society teaching self-restraint to youth awash in a culture of narcissism and sexual permissiveness."

But even the Heritage study acknowledges that abstinence pledges are not a foolproof method of protection. The study finds that few pledgers follow through on their pledges; since most are made in an individual's early teenage years, there are often many years in between the time of the pledge and marriage. Also, when they do break their pledge, youths don't use condoms. According to a 2004 study by the National

Longitudinal Study of Adolescent Health, which was funded in part by the National Institute of Child Health and Human Development and the Centers for Disease Control and Prevention, teens who take an abstinence pledge have the same rates of STDs as those who don't take pledges. "The message is really simple: 'Just say no' may work in the short term but doesn't work in the long term," states Peter Bearman, the chair of Columbia University's Sociology Department and the coauthor of the study.

The controversy over abstinence pledges is just one topic covered in the following chapter. The authors present a variety of viewpoints on what individuals can do to fight the spread of STDs.

"*Virginity pledge programs . . . have a strong and significant effect in encouraging positive and constructive behavior among youth.*"

Teens Should Take Virginity Pledges

Robert E. Rector, Kirk A. Johnson, and Jennifer A. Marshall

In the following viewpoint, Robert E. Rector, Kirk A. Johnson, and Jennifer A. Marshall argue that teens who make virginity pledges show less propensity to indulge in the risky sexual behaviors that cause sexually transmitted diseases and teen pregnancy. Concluding that there are no negative risky behaviors associated with taking a virginity pledge, the authors contend that teens have everything to gain and nothing to lose from taking a virginity pledge. Rector is a senior research fellow in domestic policy at the Heritage Foundation; Johnson is a senior policy analyst at the foundation's Center for Data Analysis, and Marshall is director of domestic policy studies at the foundation.

As you read, consider the following questions:

1. What do the authors mean when they say that teens have better life outcomes if they take a virginity pledge?

2. What does the National Longitudinal Study of Adolescent Health show about the success of abstinence pledges, according to Rector, Johnson, and Marshall?

3. According to the authors, what are factors that undermine the message of teen abstinence?

Adolescents who take a virginity pledge have substantially lower levels of sexual activity and better life outcomes when compared with similar adolescents who do not make such a pledge, according to ... data from the National Longitudinal Study of Adolescent Health (Add Health survey). Specifically, adolescents who make a virginity pledge:

- Are less likely to experience teen pregnancy;

- Are less likely to be sexually active while in high school and as young adults;

- Are less likely to give birth as teens or young adults;

- Are less likely to give birth out of wedlock;

- Are less likely to engage in risky unprotected sex; and

- Will have fewer sexual partners.

In addition, making a virginity pledge is not associated with any long-term negative outcomes. For example, teen pledgers who do become sexually active are not less likely to use contraception.

Data from the National Longitudinal Study of Adolescent Health, which is funded by more than 17 federal agencies, show that the behavior of adolescents who have made a virginity pledge is significantly different from that of peers who have not made a pledge. Teenage girls who have taken a virginity pledge are one-third less likely to experience a pregnancy before age 18. Girls who are strong pledgers (defined as those who are consistent in reporting a virginity pledge in the succeeding waves of the Add Health survey) are more than 50 percent less likely to have a teen pregnancy than are non-pledgers.

Teens who make a virginity pledge are far less likely to be sexually active during high school years. Nearly two-thirds of teens who have never taken a pledge are sexually active before age 18; by contrast, only 30 percent of teens who consistently report having made a pledge become sexually active before age 18.

Teens who have made a virginity pledge have almost half as many lifetime sexual partners as non-pledgers have. By the time they reach their early twenties, non-pledgers have had, on average, six different sex partners; pledgers, by contrast, have had three.

Girls who have taken a virginity pledge are one-third less likely to have an out-of-wedlock birth when compared with those who have never taken a pledge. Girls who are strong pledgers (those who are consistent in reporting a virginity pledge in the succeeding waves of the Add Health survey) are half as likely to have an out-of-wedlock birth as are non-pledgers.

Girls who make a virginity pledge also have fewer births overall (both marital and nonmarital) as teens and young adults than do girls who do not make pledges. By the time they reach their early twenties, some 27.2 percent of the young women who have never made a virginity pledge have given birth. By contrast, the overall birth rate of peers who have made a pledge is nearly one-third lower, at 19.8 percent.

Because they are less likely to be sexually active, pledging teens are less likely to engage in unprotected sex, especially unprotected nonmarital sex. For example, 28 percent of non-pledging youth reported engaging in unprotected nonmarital sex during the past year, compared with 22 percent of all pledgers and 17 percent of strong pledgers.

One possible explanation for the differences in behavior between pledgers and non-pledgers is that the two groups differ in important social background factors such as socioeconomic status, race, religiosity, and school performance. It is possible that these background factors—rather than the pledge *per se*—account for the differences in sexual behavior and birth rates.

To investigate this possibility, the authors performed multivariate regression analyses that compared individuals who were identical in relevant background factors. These analyses show that, although the magnitude of the differences was reduced somewhat, differences in the behavior of pledging and non-pledging teens persisted even when background factors such as socioeconomic status, race, religiosity, and other relevant variables were held constant.

Overall, making a virginity pledge is strongly associated with a wide array of positive behaviors and outcomes while having no negative effects. The findings presented in this [viewpoint] strongly suggest that virginity pledge and similar abstinence education programs have the potential to substantially reduce teen sexual activity, teen pregnancy, and out-of-wedlock childbearing.

Lower Rates of Unprotected Sexual Activity

Pledgers are significantly less likely than non-pledgers to engage in unprotected sexual activity (i.e., to have intercourse without contraception). While previous reports have suggested that sexually active pledgers are less likely to use contraception than non-pledgers are, examination of the Wave III data of the Add Health survey does not confirm this. In fact, . . . pledgers who are sexually active are slightly more likely to use contraception than are their counterparts among the non-pledging group. However, the difference between the groups is not statistically significant.

Types of Virginity Pledges

Some virginity pledges are actual signed contracts, while other "pledging" takes place at large youth rallies or even at the summer Olympics. Pledges are often developed and sponsored by religious organizations or parent groups. But all pledges have the same goal—to promote virginity until marriage.

Elisa Klein, "The Truth About Virginity Pledges," Teenwire.com, May 11, 2004. www.teenwire.com.

Conclusion

Teens who make virginity pledges promise to remain virgins until marriage. While many pledgers fail to meet that goal, as a group, teens who make virginity pledges have substantially improved behaviors compared with non-pledgers. Teens who make pledges have better life outcomes and are far less likely to engage in risky behaviors. As a whole, teen pledgers will have fewer sexual partners and are less likely to become sexually active in high school. Pledgers are less likely to experience teen pregnancy, less likely to give birth out of wedlock, and less likely to engage in unprotected sexual activity. These positive outcomes are linked to the act of making the pledge itself and are not the result of social background factors.

In addition, there are no negative risky behaviors associated with taking a virginity pledge. For example, pledgers who become sexually active are not less likely to use contraception. Thus, teens have everything to gain and nothing to lose from virginity pledge programs. Such programs appear to have a strong and significant effect in encouraging positive and constructive behavior among youth.

Today's teens, however, live in a sex-saturated culture, and positive influences that counteract the tide of permissiveness are scattered and weak. Relatively few youth are exposed to the affirmative messages coming from virginity pledge programs and similar abstinence education programs. Sadly, despite polls showing that nearly all parents want youth to be taught a strong abstinence message, abstinence education is rare in American schools. While it is true that, bowing to popular pressure, most current sex education curricula claim that they promote abstinence, in reality, these programs pay little more than lip service to the topic. Most, in fact, are permeated by anti-abstinence themes.

Still, parents continue to support abstinence values and to realize that good abstinence education programs can positively affect youth behavior. It is regrettable that most schools fail to meet either parents' expectations or students' needs.

| "Young people who take so-called 'virginity pledges' have the same rates of sexually transmitted disease (STD) as young people who do not pledge abstinence."

Virginity Pledges Have Not Reduced the Spread of STDs

Sexuality Information and Education Council of the United States

In the following viewpoint, the Sexuality Information and Education Council of the United States (SIECUS) examines the results of the National Longitudinal Study of Adolescent Health study on the rate of sexually transmitted disease (STD) infection among adolescents who take a virginity pledge and those who do not. The authors maintain that there is little correlation between the number of young people pledging in a community and actual abstinence. The Sexuality Information and Education Council of the United States is a national organization that promotes comprehensive sex education and sexual health.

Sexuality Information and Education Council of the United States, "Just Say No: Study Shows Virginity Pledgers Have Same STD Rates as Non-Pledgers," http://www.siecus.org/policy/pupdates/pdate0094.html, March 2004. Reproduced by permission of Sexuality Information and Education Council of the U.S., Inc., 130 West 42nd St., Ste. 350, New York, NY 10036.

As you read, consider the following questions:

1. What does the National Longitudinal Study of Adolescent Health show about the rate of STD infection among abstinence pledgers?
2. What is the difference in condom use between pledgers and nonpledgers, according to SIECUS?
3. What percentage of pledgers does SIECUS report eventually participated in premarital sex?

In [a] study [showing] that simply telling young people to say "no" to pre-marital sex is an insufficient public health policy, Dr. Peter Bearman, of Columbia University, and Dr. Hannah Brückner, of Yale University, have concluded that young people who take so-called "virginity pledges" have the same rates of sexually transmitted disease (STD) as young people who do not pledge abstinence. Virginity pledges, promises to abstain from all sexual activity until marriage, are the cornerstone of many federally-funded abstinence-only-until-marriage programs (both domestic and international).
. . .

For their study, Bearman and Brückner culled data from the National Longitudinal Study of Adolescent Health on a nationally representative group of 12,000 young people, ages 18–24. While Bearman and Brückner found that pledgers delayed initiation of sex, married earlier than non-pledgers, had fewer sexual partners, and were exposed to STD risk for shorter durations than non-pledgers—all statistics that should reasonably lead to lower STD rates for pledgers—in fact, STD rates for pledgers are "not statistically different than [those] for non-pledgers." Bearman presented these findings at the National STD Prevention Conference in Philadelphia, PA, on March 9, 2004.

According to the study, condom usage, or lack thereof, played an important role in STD acquisition rates. Only 40% of males who took virginity pledges used condoms compared

Virginity Pledges Are Not the Answer

Far from providing a solution to the complex problem of unintended pregnancy and STDs, pledges are undermining the use of contraception and disease-prevention methods among teens, potentially exposing them to greater harm. This is a recipe for disaster for public health in the United States.

SIECUS, "'I Swear I Won't: A Brief Explanation
of Virginity Pledges," 2005.

to 60% of their non-pledging peers. Similarly, 55% of non-pledging females used condoms, compared to only 47% of pledging females.

Young adults who took virginity pledges were also less likely than non-pledgers to consult a doctor because of STD concerns or to get tested for STDs. Therefore, they were less likely to know they were infected, and thus at greater risk of both unknowingly infecting a partner and themselves by creating a situation for increased infection by another pathogen.

Breaking the Pledge

The study also reaffirmed earlier findings that young pledgers often break their promises to remain sexually abstinent until marriage. While 99% of non-pledgers have sex before being married, 88% of young people who do take a virginity pledge also engage in premarital sex.

"This study clearly demonstrates that it is critical for us to provide all our young people with open, honest, and medically accurate information to protect themselves against STDs," said Tamara Kreinin, President and CEO of the Sexuality Information and Education Council of the U.S. (SIECUS). "It is time for lawmakers, including President [George W.] Bush, to stop using young people for political purposes and stand up for their health and their futures."

Proponents of virginity pledges responded to the study by saying that "virtually no one in the abstinence movement advocates virginity pledges as an end in themselves; pledges are simply a first step in a much longer and more involved educational process."

"Signing a pledge card does not mean you are magically protected," said Jimmy Hester, a spokesperson for the abstinence-only-until-marriage program True Love Waits. Hester also suggested that the religious foundation of the True Love Waits virginity pledges fosters a stronger commitment to abstinence. "True Love Waits is more effective than most abstinence programs that use the signing of commitment cards because it adds an element they lack—a commitment to God," Hester said. "True Love Waits would support any program that promotes abstinence, but [it] also would question the power of these types of pledges to shape long-term decisions."

True Love Waits estimates that 2.4 million young people have signed their commitment cards, which state, "Believing that true love waits, I make a commitment to God, myself, my family, my friends, my future mate, and my future children to be sexually abstinent from this day until the day I enter a biblical marriage relationship."

Religious Context

While Bearman and Brückner did not look at the religious context of virginity pledges, they did uncover a relationship between the number of young people pledging in a community and STD rates. Their previous work showed that if either too many, or too few, adolescents took virginity pledges within a community, then those pledges were not effective in helping young people delay sexual intercourse. This most recent study showed that in communities where there are too many pledgers, overall STD rates were significantly higher than in other settings. According to the study, in communities where more than 20% of young adults had taken virginity pledges, STD rates were 8.9% (for pledgers and non-pledgers) compared to 5.5% in communities with few pledgers.

According to Bearman, "Where there are too many pledgers, people misperceive risk. . . . Because pledgers make a public pledge, the sex that they have is more likely to be hidden. It is also more likely to be unsafe. The combination of hidden sex and unsafe sex fuels the absence of knowledge that pledgers and others have about the real risk of STDs."

Bearman concluded, "In this regard, just saying no, without understanding risk or how to protect oneself from risk, turns out to create greater risk and heightened STD acquisition than should be the case. Pledging does not protect young adults from STDs; in fact, in some contexts it increases their risk and the risk for others."

"The ability of latex condoms to prevent transmission of HIV has been scientifically established in 'real-life' studies ... as well as in laboratory studies."

Individuals Should Use Condoms to Prevent STDs

Centers for Disease Control and Prevention

In the following viewpoint, the Centers for Disease Control and Prevention (CDC) presents up-to-date information on the efficacy of condoms to prevent sexually transmitted disease (STD) transmission. Many studies show that condoms reduce rates of transmission of many STDs, the CDC claims. Founded in 1946, the Centers for Disease Control and Prevention is one of the thirteen major operating components of the Department of Health and Human Services, which is the principal agency of the United States government for protecting the health and safety of all Americans.

As you read, consider the following questions:

1. According to the CDC, do latex condoms prevent the

Centers for Disease Control and Prevention, "Male Latex Condoms and STDs Prevention," fact sheet for public health personnel, January 23, 2003. Reproduced by permission.

spread of HIV?

2. Are condoms more effective against some STDs than others, according to the CDC?

3. What is the best way to protect yourself from an STD, according to the CDC?

In June 2000, the National Institutes of Health (NIH), in collaboration with the Centers for Disease Control and Prevention (CDC), the Food and Drug Administration (FDA), and the United States Agency for International Development (USAID), convened a workshop to evaluate the published evidence establishing the effectiveness of latex male condoms in preventing STDs, including HIV. A summary report from that workshop was completed in July 2001 (http://www.niaid.nih.gov/dmid/stds/condomreport.pdf). This [viewpoint] is based on the NIH workshop report and additional studies that were not reviewed in that report or were published subsequent to the workshop. ... Most epidemiologic studies comparing rates of STD transmission between condom users and non-users focus on penile-vaginal intercourse.

Recommendations concerning the male latex condom and the prevention of sexually transmitted diseases (STDs), including human immunodeficiency virus (HIV), are based on information about how different STDs are transmitted, the physical properties of condoms, the anatomic coverage or protection that condoms provide, and epidemiologic studies of condom use and STD risk.

The surest way to avoid transmission of sexually transmitted diseases is to abstain from sexual intercourse, or to be in a long-term mutually monogamous relationship with a partner who has been tested and you know is uninfected.

Condoms Can Reduce the Risk of Infection

For persons whose sexual behaviors place them at risk for STDs, correct and consistent use of the male latex condom can reduce the risk of STD transmission. However, no protective method is 100 percent effective, and condom use cannot guarantee absolute protection against any STD. Furthermore, condoms lubricated with spermicides are no more effective than other lubricated condoms in protecting against the transmission of HIV and other STDs. In order to achieve the protective effect of condoms, they must be used correctly and consistently. Incorrect use can lead to condom slippage or breakage, thus diminishing their protective effect. Inconsistent use, e.g., failure to use condoms with every act of intercourse, can lead to STD transmission because transmission can occur with a single act of intercourse.

While condom use has been associated with a lower risk of cervical cancer, the use of condoms should not be a substitute for routine screening with Pap smears to detect and prevent cervical cancer.

Preventing STDs, Including HIV

Latex condoms, when used consistently and correctly, are highly effective in preventing transmission of HIV, the virus that causes AIDS. In addition, correct and consistent use of latex condoms can reduce the risk of other sexually transmitted diseases (STDs), including discharge and genital ulcer diseases. While the effect of condoms in preventing human papillomavirus (HPV) infection is unknown, condom use has been associated with a lower rate of cervical cancer, an HPV-associated disease.

How STDs Are Transmitted

There are two primary ways that STDs can be transmitted. Human immunodeficiency virus (HIV), as well as gonorrhea, chlamydia, and trichomoniasis—the discharge diseases—are transmitted when infected semen or vaginal fluids contact mucosal surfaces (e.g., the male urethra, the vagina or cervix). In contrast, genital ulcer diseases—genital herpes, syphilis, and chancroid—and human papillomavirus are primarily transmitted through contact with infected skin or mucosal surfaces.

Laboratory studies have demonstrated that latex condoms provide an essentially impermeable barrier to particles the size of STD pathogens. . . .

Condoms can be expected to provide different levels of protection for various sexually transmitted diseases, depending on differences in how the diseases are transmitted. Because condoms block the discharge of semen or protect the male urethra against exposure to vaginal secretions, a greater level of protection is provided for the discharge diseases. A lesser degree of protection is provided for the genital ulcer diseases or HPV because these infections may be transmitted by exposure to areas, e.g., infected skin or mucosal surfaces, that are not covered or protected by the condom.

Epidemiologic studies seek to measure the protective effect of condoms by comparing rates of STDs between condom users and nonusers in real-life settings. Developing such measures of condom effectiveness is challenging. Because these studies involve private behaviors that investigators cannot observe directly, it is difficult to determine accurately whether an individual is a condom user or whether condoms are used consistently and correctly. Likewise, it can be difficult to determine the level of exposure to STDs among study participants. These problems are often compounded in studies that employ a "retrospective" design, e.g., studies that measure behaviors and risks in the past.

As a result, observed measures of condom effectiveness may be inaccurate. Most epidemiologic studies of STDs, other than HIV, are characterized by these methodological limitations, and thus, the results across them vary widely—ranging from demonstrating no protection to demonstrating substantial protection associated with condom use. This inconclusiveness of epidemiologic data about condom effectiveness indicates that more research is needed—not that latex condoms do not work. For HIV infection, unlike other STDs, a number of carefully conducted studies, employing more rigorous methods and measures, have demonstrated that consistent condom use is a highly effective means of preventing HIV transmission.

Studies Support Condom Use

Another type of epidemiologic study involves examination of STD rates in populations rather than individuals. Such studies have demonstrated that when condom use increases within population groups, rates of STDs decline in these groups. Other studies have examined the relationship between condom use and the complications of sexually transmitted infections. For example, condom use has been associated with a decreased risk of cervical cancer—an HPV associated disease.

The following includes specific information for HIV, discharge diseases, genital ulcer diseases and human papillomavirus, including information on laboratory studies, the theoretical basis for protection and epidemiologic studies.

HIV/AIDS

AIDS is, by far, the most deadly sexually transmitted disease, and considerably more scientific evidence exists regarding condom effectiveness for prevention of HIV infection than for other STDs. The body of research on the effectiveness of latex condoms in preventing sexual transmission of HIV is both comprehensive and conclusive. In fact, the ability of latex condoms to prevent transmission of HIV has been scientifically established in "real-life" studies of sexually active couples as well as in laboratory studies.

Laboratory studies have demonstrated that latex condoms provide an essentially impermeable barrier to particles the size of STD pathogens. . . .

Condoms Protect Human Health

Condoms are the best protection when enjoying sexual intercourse. Condoms help make sex last longer. Condoms help prevent premature ejaculation.

Latex and female condoms reduce the risk of

- vaginitis caused by trichomoniasis
- chlamydia
- syphilis
- PID [pelvic inflammatory disease]
- chancroid
- gonorrhea
- HIV/AIDS

Latex and female condoms may offer more limited protection against

- bacterial vaginosis
- CMV [cytomegalovirus]
- genital warts
- herpes
- hepatitis B
- cervical cancer

But do not use male and female condoms together.

Jon Knowles, "Sex: Safer and Satisfying,"
Planned Parenthood of America, April 2004.
www.plannedparenthood.org.

Latex condoms cover the penis and provide an effective barrier to exposure to secretions such as semen and vaginal fluids, blocking the pathway of sexual transmission of HIV infection.

Epidemiologic studies that are conducted in real-life settings, where one partner is infected with HIV and the other partner is not, demonstrate conclusively that the consistent use of latex condoms provides a high degree of protection.

Other Diseases

Gonorrhea, chlamydia, and trichomoniasis are termed discharge diseases because they are sexually transmitted by genital secretions, such as semen or vaginal fluids. HIV is also transmitted by genital secretions.

Laboratory studies have demonstrated that latex condoms provide an essentially impermeable barrier to particles the size of STD pathogens. . . .

The physical properties of latex condoms protect against discharge diseases such as gonorrhea, chlamydia, and trichomoniasis, by providing a barrier to the genital secretions that transmit STD-causing organisms.

Epidemiologic studies that compare infection rates among condom users and nonusers provide evidence that latex condoms can protect against the transmission of chlamydia, gonorrhea and trichomoniasis. However, some other epidemiologic studies show little or no protection against these infections. Many of the available epidemiologic studies were not designed or conducted in ways that allow for accurate measurement of condom effectiveness against the discharge diseases. More research is needed to assess the degree of protection latex condoms provide for discharge diseases, other than HIV.

Genital Ulcer Diseases

Genital ulcer diseases include genital herpes, syphilis, and chancroid. These diseases are transmitted primarily through "skin-to-skin" contact from sores/ulcers or infected skin that looks normal. HPV infections are transmitted through contact with infected genital skin or mucosal surfaces/fluids. Genital ulcer diseases and HPV infection can occur in male or female genital areas that are, or are not, covered (protected by the condom).

Laboratory studies have demonstrated that latex condoms provide an essentially impermeable barrier to particles the size of STD pathogens. . . .

Protection against genital ulcer diseases and HPV depends on the site of the sore/ulcer or infection. Latex condoms can only protect against transmission when the ulcers or infections are in genital areas that are covered or protected by the condom. Thus, consistent and correct use of latex condoms would be expected to protect against transmission of genital ulcer diseases and HPV in some, but not all, instances.

Epidemiologic studies that compare infection rates among condom users and nonusers provide evidence that latex condoms can protect against the transmission of syphilis and genital herpes. However, some other epidemiologic studies show little or no protection. Many of the available epidemiologic studies were not designed or conducted in ways that allow for accurate measurement of condom effectiveness against the genital ulcer diseases. No conclusive studies have specifically addressed the transmission of chancroid and condom use, although several studies have documented a reduced risk of genital ulcers in settings where chancroid is a leading cause of genital ulcers. More research is needed to assess the degree of protection latex condoms provide for the genital ulcer diseases.

While some epidemiologic studies have demonstrated lower rates of HPV infection among condom users, most have not. It is particularly difficult to study the relationship between condom use and HPV infection because HPV infection is often intermittently detectable and because it is difficult to assess the frequency of either existing or new infections. Many of the available epidemiologic studies were not designed or conducted in ways that allow for accurate measurement of condom effectiveness against HPV infection.

A number of studies, however, do show an association between condom use and a reduced risk of HPV-associated diseases, including genital warts, cervical dysplasia and cervical cancer. The reason for lower rates of cervical cancer among condom users observed in some studies is unknown. HPV infection is believed to be required, but not by itself sufficient, for cervical cancer to occur. Co-infections with other STDs may be a factor in increasing the likelihood that HPV infection will lead to cervical cancer. More research is needed to assess the degree of protection latex condoms provide for both HPV infection and HPV-associated disease, such as cervical cancer.

| "Condoms, the only form of birth control purported to stop disease and the spread of STDs, don't work."

The Benefits of Condom Use Are Exaggerated

Angie Vineyard

In the following viewpoint, Angie Vineyard argues that condoms are not as effective in protecting teens against the transmission of sexually transmitted diseases (STDs) as media reports suggest. She contends that teens should be embracing abstinence as a sure method to remain free of HIV and other STDs. Vineyard is a research fellow at the Beverly LaHaye Institute: A Center for Studies in Women's Issues, which is the research division of the Concerned Women for America (CFA). CFA is a conservative Christian women's policy organization.

As you read, consider the following questions:

1. How many teens does Vineyard say are infected with an STD every day?
2. Do condoms work to prevent STD transmission, in the author's view?

Angie Vineyard, "Protection Teens Are Still Not Getting," www.cwfa.org, December 19, 2002. Reproduced by permission.

3. What is Project Reality, according to Vineyard?

The numbers are nothing short of staggering.

Every day, 8,000 teens will become infected with a new STD. One STD, herpes, has skyrocketed 500% in the last 20 years among White American teenagers. In fact, one in five children over age 12 tests positive for herpes type 2, which has no cure. Almost 50% of African-American teenagers have genital herpes, also with no cure. Nearly one out of ten teenage girls has chlamydia and half of all newly diagnosed chlamydia cases are in girls 15 to 19 years old.

This is not a crisis. It's an epidemic. And that's exactly what Dr. Meg Meeker has titled her book, "*Epidemic: How Teen Sex is Killing Our Kids.*"

Having treated thousands of patients for 20 years, Meeker found an enormous surge in STDs not just with low-income teens but also with teens from middle and higher-income families. And while a shot of penicillin four decades ago cured the only two known STDs, syphilis and gonorrhea, today the CDC [Centers for Disease Control and Prevention] has identified at least 25 STDs and termed this frightening trend a "multiple" epidemic.

Meeker puts faces on the harrowing numbers by weaving first-hand patient accounts with shocking statistics. Lori, taken into the emergency room with a high fever and intense abdominal pain, was initially diagnosed with acute appendicitis. She had a life threatening case of pelvic inflammatory disease, caused by either chlamydia or gonorrhea. While Lori pulled through, she will probably never bear children. Alex contracted genital herpes at the age of 17. A year later, he had sunk into such a deep depression that he became suicidal. And then there's Heather, who despite using oral contraceptives, contracted human papilloma virus, HPV, and at 19, was diagnosed with cervical cancer and had to have part of her cervix removed.

Condoms Do Not Work

On July 20, 2001, a report was issued by the U.S. Department of Health and Human Services. A scientific panel co-sponsored by the National Institutes of Health (NIH), the Food and Drug Administration (FDA), the Centers for Disease Control and Prevention (CDC), the U.S. Agency for International Development (USAID), developed the report. It was based on a yearlong study in which 28 researchers reviewed 138 peer-reviewed, published studies on the heterosexual transmission of sexually transmitted diseases (STD).

Their findings were stunning. Basically, it boils down to this: There is no evidence to indicate that condoms prevent the heterosexual transmission of most sexually transmitted diseases. None.

Mary Beth Bonacci, Catholic Herald, *September 6, 2001.*

The Condom Myth

Sadly, these teens bought into the prevailing cultural myth. For decades, we've held up that shiny foil packet as the quick-fix solution for our hormone-driven adolescents. Kids have been told that, of course, they are going to have sex and they need protection. They need a condom. And they've listened. Condom use among adolescents has soared in recent years. Public officials gushed when they learned that condom use among sexually active teen boys has jumped from 21% to a whopping 67% in the last 20 years. The condom indoctrination has worked!

But while condom use has reduced the risk for teen pregnancy and the spread of HIV, the National Institutes of Health declared that there was not enough evidence to determine that male latex condoms were effective in reducing the risk of most other sexually transmitted diseases. HPV, the fastest growing STD in America today is directly responsible for 99.7% of cervical cancer cases. But the NIH's Condom Report stated that "condoms have no impact on the risk of sexual transmission of human papilloma virus in women."

Meeker writes, "Condoms, the only form of birth control purported to stop disease and the spread of STDs, don't work. (They) have lulled us into complacency too long. They have provided a stopgap measure that can no longer hold back the flood of STDs. Our reliance on condoms has played a key role in the spread of disease."

Meeker has not been tapped by the Bush Administration to push abstinence-only education in America's public schools. She is not a conservative spokesperson for pro-family organizations paid to decry the ills of risky sexual behavior and condom distribution. She is a physician, who stares into the eyes of scared teenagers every day, telling them they have STDs that are incurable and helping them cope with the depression that ensues. She has placed herself on the front lines of this sexual revolution and she's cleaning up the mess we've made in telling our teenagers that sex is O.K., as long as they wear a condom.

But physicians aren't the only ones noticing this epidemic. Teachers are also paying attention. . . . The Philadelphia, PA school district announced it would offer free screenings and treatment to more than 50,000 students for STDs. Officials estimate that in [one] month . . . alone, 3,000 teens in this district will test positive for chlamydia, which if left untreated, can lead to infertility or be passed on to newborns.

Perhaps this epidemic is what propels people like Scott Phelps to alert teachers and students nationwide to the pitfalls of STDs, the empty promise of "safe" sex and the benefits of abstinence.

"You're 16 or 17 years old and you get genital herpes. Has no cure. (You) have it for the rest of your life. When you're 26, 27 and you meet someone you want to marry, you're all excited. Is the herpes going to be a problem?" he asked at a Washington D.C. teacher training session sponsored by the non-profit abstinence group, Project Reality. "Abstinence is about freedom, to live your life and your future the way you want to live it without having to get handcuffed and drag that stuff with you for the rest of your life."

As teachers scribbled down notes, one school nurse paid special attention to the statistics given. Having worked in the D.C. area for six years, she's seen hundreds of cases of STDs and teen pregnancies. But she is part of a growing trend of teachers who are weary of the toll teen sex has taken on adolescents.

"Most of us see abstinence as a very important choice," she said, asking to remain anonymous.

[As of the end of 2002,] Project Reality's abstinence program has been taught to 42,000 students in the state of Illinois alone and is spreading to 25 other states.

Besides a renewed popularity in abstinence education, Phelps believes this epidemic will also produce a deluge of lawsuits from angry parents whose teenagers bargained for "safe" sex but got STDs instead.

"If I tell a kid 'If you're sexually active, make sure you use a condom' and he does that and he gets HPV and he comes back in 3 years and says, 'I did this'. What am I going to say? I'm going to feel responsible, guilty and liable."

> "While abstinence is anathema to the
> [gay/HIV/AIDS] advocacy groups, they
> can at least preach restraint and
> responsibility."

Gay Men Should Take Responsibility for Their Sexual Practices

Katherine Ernst

In the following viewpoint, Katherine Ernst contends that gay men should be taking responsibility for a resurgence of promiscuous and irresponsible sexual behavior. Fueled by crystal meth, some gay men are participating in unsafe sex with multiple partners. Furthermore, gay advocacy groups are not providing leadership or moral guidance on the issue. She contends that these groups must stand up and stigmatize such behavior in order to reverse the increasing rates of sexually transmitted disease infection in some segments of the gay population. Ernst is a writer for City Journal, *a publication of the Manhattan Institute in New York City.*

Katherine Ernst, "AIDS, Sex, and Drugs," www.manhattan-institute.org, February 18, 2005. Reproduced by permission.

As you read, consider the following questions:

1. What kind of high-risk behavior does Ernst say some gay men are indulging in that leaves them more vulnerable to being infected with an STD?

2. What is crystal meth and how does it affect sexual inhibitions, according to Ernst?

3. How have gay advocacy groups responded to the fact that some gay men are participating in irresponsible sexual behavior, in the author's view?

In the past quarter century, HIV/AIDS has made a dramatic shift in the way it manifests itself in the American psyche. Gone are the scary *Time* magazine cover stories and brooding black-and-white public service commercials; now we have U2's Bono, serenading infected orphans a few continents away (while asking the First World to contribute money for relief). So when a new Überstrain of the virus—progressing to full-blown AIDS in a matter of months and immune to 19 of the 20 drugs available for treatment—was discovered in a New York City man, public health officials and the media took notice. Suddenly, AIDS was in our own backyard again.

This new strain, dubbed "3-DCR HIV," may be much ado about nothing—an isolated case related to one particular person's immune system—or the start of a public health nightmare (researchers believe they have found a similar strain in a San Diego man). Regardless, the circumstances surrounding the man's infection offer an alarming glimpse into part of New York's gay subculture and its related advocacy groups.

To begin, the anonymous patient is a 40-something gay man who, according to a *New York Times* source briefed on the case, engaged in unprotected sex with "hundreds" (yes, that's "hundreds" with an "s") of partners [in 2004]. Oh, and he was using crystal meth at the same time. This is not risky behavior; it's downright self-destructive behavior that, sadly, is part of a trend in New York City.

Dangerous Attitudes

When asked what his responsibility to a sexual partner is, Mark, an HIV-positive gay man from Texas who declined to reveal his real name, says it doesn't go further than disclosure. "My responsibility is to let them know [I am positive] and let them make their own decision since they are an adult," says Mark, who cruises Interact chat rooms for sex. He believes gay men "shouldn't be worried about HIV anymore," because medical care "has it under control."

Christopher Lisotta, Advocate, *February 17, 2004.*

Crystal Meth Use Is a Factor in STD Transmission

Crystal methamphetamine is your nightmare Bad Drug. More addictive than heroin, the central nervous system stimulant brings users to euphoric, energetic, and confident highs—if they're lucky enough not to overdose (which could trigger a stroke, heart attack, or death). "Crashing" down from this high brings not only intense physical discomfort, such as nausea, but a severe emotional drain. Users are likely to develop depression, marked by feelings of irritability, and even psychosis (the *Philadelphia Inquirer* quotes a former user: "the 'shadow people' were everywhere"). To escape from such emotional and physical distress, users thus clamor for more of the drug, and inevitably enter an upward (and downward) spiral of addiction.

The popularity of the drug (which began, surprisingly, in rural America) in the Big Apple seems to have settled "primarily among gay men"—so says the New York City Department of Health and Mental Hygiene. And the *Times* offers up some anecdotal evidence: "a recent survey of gay men found that 25 percent had tried crystal meth in the last few months." Indeed, there's no denying an element of the gay subculture in the city has taken a dangerous liking to the drug: some members of gay websites will tag themselves "PNP" ("party and play")—meaning sex with crystal meth. They even refer to the drug by cutsie nicknames, such as Tina and tweak. Tina, after all, will loosen any inhibitions they have and enable them to take part in marathon sex sessions with multiple people, many of them complete strangers. Thus, with the danger of HIV/AIDS (the Centers for Disease Control and Prevention says HIV infections rose 11 percent among gay men from 2000 to 2003, while the rest of the population's infection rate remained virtually stable) and STDs (in the last five years, syphilis cases have increased a whopping 400 percent among gay men in New York City), these men are most certainly playing with fire.

So what do the ever-present HIV/AIDS/gay advocacy groups in the city have to say about such behavior? HIV Forum NYC has been aware of the problem for well over a year and has created its own subdivision, the Crystal Meth Working Group, to educate the gay population about the drug. Their latest ad campaign: "Crystal Free and Sexy." As their website says, "the goal of the [print ad] campaign is to elevate gay men in the community that do not use crystal meth and are sexy, have fun and live full lives. They may go to clubs or not. They may use drugs or not. The one thing they all have in common is that they do not use crystal meth and they are hot, cool and hip." (Nancy Reagan should've used this: "The sexy say no to drugs.") In other words, your promiscuous, pot-smoking, gay boyfriend is cool, as long as he's not injecting some "tweak."

At least HIV Forum NYC is condemning the use of the drug. Another group, Gay Men's Health Crisis [GMHC], is another story. Their advisory, "Crystal Meth: What You Need to Know," is both comical and sad in how it attempts to avoid judgment at all costs. After explaining why gay men take the drug, what happens (written in startlingly graphic terms) when the drug is taken during gay sex, and meth's guaranteed dangers, GMHC then says, "If you are going to use, you ought to use extreme caution and limit how much you take. . . . Don't assume you didn't get enough. The more you use the less burning you will feel in your nose and the less intense you may feel. If you don't feel it right away, wait." And, "If you are injecting (slamming) crystal," they offer some more helpful tips: "Use a new syringe and new equipment every time you inject. . . . Clean injection sites with alcohol pads before injecting. If alcohol pads are not available, clean the injection site with warm soap and water." And so on.

GMHC is saying, in other words, "This stuff is bad, but if you're gonna do it, do it right." This is analogous to saying, "Teenagers are going to drink beer no matter what we do. Might as well tell 'em where to get the best fake ID." So afraid are they of being seen as judgmental, GMHC would rather inadvertently promote meth use than say to at-risk members, "Don't touch this illegal substance."

Preach Restraint and Responsibility

The dangers of crystal meth aside, both advocacy groups remain silent on an even bigger factor in HIV infections: promiscuous sex. Had the New York City man with the super-bug cut his number of partners down to, say, *single digits*, he might not be making headlines today. While abstinence is anathema to the advocacy groups, they can at least preach restraint and responsibility. But no: better to stay silent than to be seen as prudish or even—eek!—socially conservative. (The *New York Times*, normally in thrall to PC orthodoxy on gay issues, has been comparatively sensible in its coverage of this problem.)

This is not to say that if a few HIV/AIDS/gay advocacy groups change their ad campaigns or the contents of their websites, New York City will be HIV-free. But personal responsibility will go much farther in the fight against AIDS than waiting around for a government-subsidized cure. It would behoove the advocacy groups to catch up with the rest of society and put a stigma, as scary as it might be for them, on the irresponsible behavior that leads to HIV/AIDS, other diseases, and broken lives. Such a stigma would lower the risk of another 1980s-style outbreak. Even the sexy would approve.

> *"Young gay men coming out into the current atmosphere of fear, resentment, and superficiality can hardly be blamed for an inability to make healthy sexual decisions."*

Accusing Gay Men of Irresponsible Sexual Practices Is Counterproductive

Patrick Moore

In the following viewpoint, Patrick Moore acknowledges that the gay community has to address the problems of rampant crystal meth use and its link to the increase in HIV rates among gay men. To do this, he argues, they must first confront the crippling self-loathing related to gay sexuality that is only intensified by accusations of irresponsible sex practices. He then recommends contacting sexually active men in places they frequent, such as bathhouses and sex clubs, in order to efficiently provide education and leadership on the issue. Moore is a novelist and journalist who writes extensively on gay issues.

As you read, consider the following questions:

1. According to the author, why is self-loathing such a serious problem in the gay community, and how does it affect sexual behavior?

2. How should the gay community deal with the crystal meth problem, in the author's view?

3. How does crystal meth make gay men more susceptible to HIV transmission, in Moore's view?

After enduring decades of devastation, the gay community is now witnessing a new generation of young men becoming infected with HIV, seemingly oblivious to the death and suffering that they might have escaped. We also see middle-aged gay men, having survived HIV thus far, endangering both themselves and others with unsafe sex. We are told that this phenomenon is largely the result of a new crisis: crystal meth addiction. But crystal abuse is only one symptom of a malady called self-loathing, which feeds on the denial, separatism, sexual repression, and untreated grief that now permeate gay life in America.

It is no coincidence that gay crystal use began to expand rapidly at about the same time that "the cocktail" began to make HIV seem like less of a death sentence, throwing many gay men back into life with absolutely no preparation. Men who had assumed their lives were over had to find new ways to feel erotic and vital while coping with grief, shock, and the heavy side effects of their medications. The emotional impact of AIDS on their lives left these men with little investment in their own future, let alone that of the [HIV-]negative men with whom they were having sex. For a few hours or days, crystal's intensity could erase the pain of the past and the fear of the future.

Many older men who had somehow escaped HIV infection but had watched loved ones die in their arms were equally damaged and disconnected. The rituals of marches, funerals, and volunteering had suddenly stopped, taking with them much of the sense of unity that had marked the '80s and early '90s. Alone again, we were expected to pick up the shards of our shattered lives. Crystal, along with other drugs and alcohol, offered a chemically induced sense of belonging.

The Aftermath of the AIDS Crisis

As a community, we haven't yet figured out how to make sense of what happened to us during the first decades of the AIDS crisis, let alone come to terms with the fact that it is still happening. We just want to move on. We are lacking in new spiritual rituals, targeted services, and the honesty that might help us deal with our grief. Most gay men age 40 and under have lived their entire adult sexual lives under the shadow of AIDS, forever linking sex and self-destructiveness in our minds. Yet we have no public spaces to discuss these messages because we rarely discuss sex anymore. Gay sex is now seen either in terms of monogamous marriage or shameful promiscuity. Our sexual self-repression (as reflected in media images of neutered gay men) creates an atmosphere of fear and shame around sex that stifles healthy exploration.

Young gay men coming out into the current atmosphere of fear, resentment, and superficiality can hardly be blamed for an inability to make healthy sexual decisions. Their choices are clouded by the fact that crystal is widely available, costs little, and produces a kind of sexual high particularly attuned to the thrilling self-destructiveness of youth. It is vital that older generations who were directly impacted by the first decades of the AIDS crisis undergo the process of understanding, in a complex and compassionate way, both our own self-destructive behavior and the reasons for the current wave of infections in the young. Without this understanding, it is entirely likely that we will close our minds, hearts, and wallets to those now becoming infected.

But compassion seems to be in short supply these days. The commercialization of gay life and the ongoing problem of racism make it easier for gay Americans to care for those suffering with HIV in Africa than to acknowledge that 10% of black gay men in America are now infected with HIV. A significant number of these men don't identify as gay, making outreach to them difficult and minimizing the kind of personal connection that characterized early AIDS services in the United States. The U.S. AIDS establishment has perpetuated the misleading and damaging message that "AIDS is no longer a gay disease." In fact, in the United States of America, gay men still make up about half of new infections. As a group with highly specific sexual problems and a record of addiction, jumping on the "We Are the World" bandwagon does not make sense in terms of the kind of research, education, and prevention gay men need here.

Dealing with the Problem

So how do we deal with the immediate crystal problem? Let's hope that we can one day acknowledge the emotional damage wrought by the AIDS crisis, develop services to deal with it, and sanction a wide range of sexual lifestyles instead of using marriage to create a system of "good gays" and "bad gays." Let's even dream of a day when the gay community and the black community will work together to help young black gay men feel that they are of value. Both strategies could begin to eliminate the systemic disease of self-loathing that creates addiction.

As for immediate education efforts, the straightforward message of condom use that many AIDS organizations currently broadcast is not wrong so much as it is simplistic. Most agencies remain wary of explicitly addressing how men who are using drugs actually have sex. Nearly 25 years into the AIDS crisis, gay men are well aware that condoms prevent HIV transmission, but all of the safe sex knowledge in the

Crystal Meth Is a Symptom, Not the Problem

I suggest that crystal meth addiction is one of the symptoms of a lingering "community depression" due to unacknowledged or under-acknowledged losses from AIDS. Could the three-day sex/crystal binges, in a half-unconscious state, be the result of the emotional de-humanization of ourselves in a world where our lives—and deaths—are susceptible to being trashed, minimized, or devalued? . . . Many gay men have lost friends and lovers to AIDS. I often wonder whether these losses have been honored as they should. Also, in addition to medical and psychosocial grief created by the disease, many gay men feel ashamed and guilty for contracting HIV or developing AIDS, which is still a taboo subject. Could crystal meth addiction be a sign of our unacknowledged suffering?

Jean Malpas, Body Positive, *October 2004.*

world is beside the point when you've been up for three days on crystal and self-destruction has become the world's biggest turn-on.

Viable education programs do already exist and must be expanded. During the time I served on the board of the Van Ness Recovery House in Los Angeles, I learned a fundamental lesson from Kathy Watt, the program's executive director. She told me, "We operate on the assumption that people should have the opportunity to have the sexual experience they are looking for, but in a safer way. We need to meet them where they're at."

HIV infection results from crystal not just because gay men are out of control but also because of the physical conditions specific to crystal use. Men on crystal often have mouth sores from grinding their teeth, for example, and oral transmission of HIV is more likely for them. That's a level of information rarely provided in prevention campaigns or mainstream research.

Community Outreach

The men we need to reach are not hanging out at the local community center. They're at the sex clubs. We cannot afford to shut down or alienate these businesses. They represent our best educational forum.

The Van Ness Recovery House works inside bathhouses and sex clubs to provide education that acknowledges drug use and helps clients negotiate safer ways of having sex in a dangerous environment. The Van Ness House also has a stringent ethics policy: Outreach workers are strictly prohibited from sexual behavior in venues where they've worked (or might work in the future) because blurring the line between participant and educator can lead to disaster. Also, the same workers staff the same club week after week so that patrons can develop a level of trust and be encouraged to discuss difficult issues. Most important: HIV prevention workers are cross-trained in drug counseling (a rarity in outreach programs) so that they can provide a message truly targeted to their clients.

If we want to deal with the crystal problem, let's deal with it immediately by expanding such existing programs. Fortunately, many of these have honesty as a core component of their effectiveness, so perhaps our efforts will have the added benefit of getting us to look more carefully at the river of problems coursing beneath the glittering surface of contemporary gay life.

Periodical Bibliography

The following articles have been selected to supplement the diverse views presented in this chapter.

Patrick J. Buchanan — "The Great Condom Fraud and Cover Up," *American Cause*, March 1, 2002.

Jordan Ellenberg — "Sex and Significance: How the Heritage Foundation Cooked the Books on Virginity," *Slate.com*, July 7, 2005. http://www.slate.com.

Tom Farley — "Cruise Control," *Washington Monthly*, November 2002.

James K. Glassman — "Sex, Religion, and AIDS," *American Enterprise Online*, September 2004. www.taemag.com.

Todd Henneman — "Scared of Sex," *Advocate*, August 17, 2004.

Christopher Lisotta — "Return of the Bug Chaser," *Advocate*, February 17, 2004.

Stuart McKee — "The Face on the Men's Room Wall," *Print*, July/August 2004.

Caryle Murphy — "Programs Help Sort Out Sex, Morality Issues," *Washington Post*, April 6, 2003.

Katha Pollitt — "Virginity or Death!" *Nation*, May 12, 2005.

Andrew Webb — "When the Rubber Hits the Road," *Washington Monthly*, November 2001.

OPPOSING
VIEWPOINTS®
SERIES

CHAPTER 4

How Should the Global AIDS Crisis Be Addressed?

Chapter Preface

The Global Fund to Fight AIDS, Tuberculosis, and Malaria reports that in 2003, about 3 million people died of AIDS worldwide, three-quarters of them in sub-Saharan Africa alone. An additional 5 million people were newly infected. Young people aged fifteen to twenty-four account for 42 percent of new HIV infections and represent almost one-third of people living with HIV/AIDS worldwide. The organization also reports that prevention programs reach fewer than one in five people who need them. More accessible prevention programs could avert 29 million of the 45 million new infections projected by 2010, the fund avers. Given the scope of the problem, many experts believe that AIDS is a matter of global concern and requires a coordinated and sustained response by the international community.

In his 2003 State of the Union address, President George W. Bush took a bold step: He announced a $15 billion, five-year program to focus on the global fight against HIV/AIDS—the largest commitment ever made by any nation to fight a disease on an international scale. Despite what appears to be a laudable commitment, however, America's contribution in the fight against HIV/AIDS has been the subject of international debate.

In 2005, the Bush administration set aside $2.3 billion for international AIDS services, which would meet only 19 percent of what the United Nations says is needed for a minimal effort to address the crisis. In defense of the U.S. contribution, Randall Tobias, the U.S. Global AIDS Coordinator, asserted in 2005 that "America is spending nearly twice as much to fight global AIDS as the rest of the world's donor governments combined. By its actions, the United States has challenged the rest of the world to take action." Most of that money, however, would be spent on initiatives that stress abstinence over condom use, which critics claim is an ineffective strategy in fighting AIDS. Critics also contend that Bush's plan has been underfunded. A Global Fund press release states that "as of [2004], the Global Fund will not have enough funding to provide any additional grants next year and will likely not be able to initiate a new round of grants until 2007. Given that 3 million people die each year from AIDS, the several-year delay in new grants will mean that many people will die that could otherwise have been treated."

While most health experts agree that global AIDS must be addressed, they often disagree on the best approach. The authors in the following chapter examine this controversy as well as others pertaining to the international battle against AIDS.

> "The United States has ... willingly
> assumed the leadership role in this
> fight [against HIV/AIDS]. ... Already
> we are seeing results."

U.S. Global AIDS Policy Is Effective

Randall Tobias

In the following viewpoint, which is excerpted from his 2004 speech at the International AIDS Conference, Randall Tobias urges a united front against AIDS. He defends U.S. efforts to fight AIDS around the world, claiming that America is leading the effort to combat AIDS. Tobias was appointed the U.S. Global AIDS Coordinator in July 2003. In that position, he coordinates international HIV/AIDS activities for all American government departments and agencies.

As you read, consider the following questions:

1. According to the author, how is the Bush administration responding to the global AIDS crisis?
2. How can pharmaceutical companies help fight the global

Randall Tobias (US Global AIDS Coordinator), 15th International AIDS Conference Speech, July 14, 2004.

AIDS crisis, in Tobias's view?

3. How much does Tobias say America is spending on fighting global AIDS in comparison to the rest of the world's donor governments?

In the past, we in the developed world displayed ignorance, or even apathy, about the global dimensions and intricacies of the AIDS crisis. Over time, I believe awareness grew and apathy turned to empathy. Empathy is important—but it is really not enough.

So I believe we all need to acknowledge the inadequacy of the world's response. But I also believe that it is time—in fact, it is past time—to move forward from this point. Too much time has been lost already.

At this point, perhaps the most critical mistake we can make is to allow this pandemic to divide us. We are striving toward the same goal—a world free of HIV/AIDS. When 8,000 lives are lost to AIDS every day, division is a luxury we cannot afford.

I recently visited Mozambique, one of the countries where the U.S. is dramatically increasing our investment. I visited a woman living in a very resource-poor setting. Tragically, she was on the verge of passing away from AIDS. Sitting on the edge of her mother's mattress was the woman's daughter, perhaps 5 years old. I asked the home-care volunteer who was present during my visit who would be taking care of that little girl when her mother was gone. She told me no one had an answer. Her father had also passed away from AIDS, and it was not clear that anyone in her extended family would be able to help.

A mother passes away.

A child is orphaned.

One family's tragedy reflects the devastation that this epidemic is bringing to bear. Every day, thousands are suffering and dying like that woman, but each one has a name.

Thousands are losing their parents—and much of their hope for a better life—like that little girl.

When I insist that we put our differences aside and focus on the real enemy, I do not ask that we do it for our own benefit. I ask that we do it for that woman, that little girl. They deserve nothing less.

The Real Enemy

Let me say this as directly as I can: HIV/AIDS is the real enemy. The denial, stigma, and complacency that fuel HIV/AIDS—these too are real enemies. It is morally imperative that we direct our energies at these enemies, not at one another. We may not agree on every tactic employed by every donor and we may have passionate opinions about how things can be done better, but we must work with each other to find the best solutions, while knowing that every person in this fight simply wants to save lives. That is a noble calling, and should be appreciated and respected.

The United States has decisively turned the corner, from the eras of apathy and empathy, to a new era of compassionate action. We have willingly assumed the leadership role in this fight. . . . Already we are seeing results. . . .

Real Results

Within days of receiving funding, we were traveling by motor scooter to deliver antiretroviral drugs [ARVs] to people in their homes in rural Uganda. Within weeks, we were doubling the number of patients on ARVs in urban Uganda. We put 500 people on therapy at just one site in Kenya. One of our treatment partners has begun therapy for another 500 patients in just two countries, and they are enrolling more patients at a rate of 220 per week. Another partner mentioned to us . . . that they will begin delivering ARVs at multiple centers, expanding to nine countries rapidly. We have ordered and are receiving drug treatments in nearly all of our focus countries.

America is providing leadership in the fight to keep HIV-positive people alive by providing antiretroviral drugs. Not just any drugs, but safe and effective drugs. I have consistently and repeatedly expressed our intent to provide, through the Emergency Plan, AIDS drugs that are acquired at the lowest possible cost, regardless of origin or who produces them, as long as we know they are safe, effective, and of high quality. These drugs may include brand-name products, generics, or copies of brand-name products.

I call on each [donor nation] to urge every company manufacturing these drugs to file their applications as soon as possible so we can begin funding these drugs as soon as possible.

At this point in the development of our bilateral plan, as well as the multilateral programs we support, the availability of drugs—though very important—is far from being the main constraint on our work. The major challenge is one that is becoming widely recognized: the need for human capacity and infrastructure that can accommodate our investment. Ignoring those limitations means wasting money and failing to solve problems. In places like Africa, the Caribbean, and Southeast Asia, there is a desperate lack of health care workers and infrastructure. African leaders understand this, sometimes better than we from the developing world do. All the AIDS drugs in the world won't do any good if they're stuck in warehouses with no place to go to actually be part of the delivery of treatment to those in need.

In the U.S., we have 279 physicians for every 100,000 people. In Mozambique, however, there are only 2.6 physicians for every 100,000 people. That means that just 500 physicians serve the needs of the entire country—a population of 18 million.

In some countries, the "brain-drain" of trained medical personnel is an enormous problem. In Ethiopia, where there are only 2.9 physicians for every 100,000 people, a physician there told me that there are more Ethiopian-trained physicians practicing today in Chicago than in all of Ethiopia.

We have to find solutions for these human resource issues, including the development of new models for the treatment and care of patients. Obviously, without making progress on the capacity issue, our ability to deliver prevention, treatment and care is quite limited. That's why . . . the President's Emergency Plan is making a tremendous investment in training and infrastructure. Improving capacity is essential for all efforts to be sustainable in these countries for the long term.

America Will Help

After 20 years fighting HIV/AIDS worldwide, America has a wealth of experience, infrastructure and relationships. Thus we are in a particularly strong position to help address the capacity issue. Our experience on the ground is allowing us both to implement our own Emergency Plan with urgency, and to assist our multinational partners, such as the Global Fund, in building their programs.

To cite just one example, the U.S. has quickly trained 14,700 health workers and built capacity at over 900 different health care sites, as part of our "prevention of mother-to-child transmission" programs in just 18 months. But let's look beyond the numbers, at what that training and capacity building has meant to one woman in Guyana.

Brenda, already a mother of one child, attended her first antenatal visit in her second pregnancy. During group counseling, her health visitor—trained by the United States—discussed transmission of HIV from mothers to infants and ways to reduce the risk of this transmission. In the individual session, Brenda, who was about twelve weeks pregnant, went through pre-test counseling on HIV, and agreed to be tested.

Brenda did not attend the clinic for two months, because she was experiencing great difficulties in finding a stable place to live, since she had severed her relationship with her partner.

U.S. Global AIDS Commitment Is the World's Largest

In the President's 2003 State of the Union address, he announced a $15 billion, five-year program to focus on HIV/AIDS. It is the largest commitment ever made by any nation for addressing an international disease state.

We are focusing on programs in 123 countries around the world, but a special focus on 15 of those countries that together account for about 50 percent of the infections in the world. Twelve of those 15 countries are in Africa. So a major focus of our attention is in Africa.

The objectives of this program in five years are to get 2 million people on antiretroviral drug treatment to save 7 million infections that otherwise would have occurred, and to provide care for 10 million people—"care" defined as people who don't yet need drug treatment, people who are at the end of life, and, very importantly, orphans, who are just a huge, huge issue here.

Randall Tobias, Press Briefing,
The White House, July 14, 2005.

During her second visit, the nurse shared her HIV test result. Unfortunately, the form was stamped "HIV antibodies detected."

That was a difficult moment—one that I know many in this room have experienced. Brenda reacted with disbelief and then hurt, as anyone would. But caring health workers calmed her, reassuring her that she could live a healthy life with HIV. When Brenda told her mother and siblings, they overcame their shock and encouraged her to go through the U.S.-supported program to protect against transmission to her child.

Brenda received further counseling at the clinic and joined a support group of HIV-positive mothers. Four hours before delivery, Brenda received the single-dose antiretroviral prophylaxis, and the baby received a pediatric dose of nevirapine. Her baby is now HIV free.

After giving birth, Brenda became an advocate and community educator for the Network of People Living with HIV/AIDS in Guyana. Brenda says, "Today, I can use myself as an example to talk to other women about HIV/AIDS. I am not ashamed of my condition, and I feel that I can use my experience to help others."

America and Its Partners

Once again, it all started with training health visitors—without those people, and the places for them to work, none of this would have been possible. That's exactly the kind of effect we want our capacity-building work to have—to save people from HIV and its effects, and to build sustainable leadership in their communities. America is proud to be a partner in building a better life for people like Brenda—and her baby.

Since I mentioned our multinational partners, let me note that bilateral U.S. programs, while a critical part of the President's Emergency Plan, are by no means all of it. Our strategy aims to increase the overall chances of success by pursuing multiple approaches to this complex emergency—supporting and partnering with individuals, community and faith-based organizations, host governments, and multilateral institutions like the Global Fund and the United Nations. We want to use every means at our disposal to address this crisis, and that is what we are doing.

The Bush Administration took the lead in helping to found the Global Fund. The U.S. Secretary of Health and Human Services, Tommy Thompson, serves as the Chairman of its Board. The Global Fund is a young venture and still maturing, but we consider it a very promising vehicle and a critically important part of the work that all of us are doing—including the implementation of the President's Emergency Plan. The U.S. is working with the Global Fund to build capacity on the ground so that more of the Fund's money can begin to flow and to reach those who need it.

America is the world's largest contributor to the Fund—making thirty-six percent of all pledges to date. The Fund offers a vehicle for other donors to substantially increase their commitment to this fight, as the United States has done.

Once again, I must speak directly. This year America is spending nearly twice as much to fight global AIDS as the rest of the world's donor governments combined. By its actions, the United States has challenged the rest of the world to take action.

> *"Delaying delivery of resources, drugs, treatments, and research has been the hallmark of the Bush policy on AIDS since 2003."*

U.S. Global AIDS Policy Is Ineffective

Joel Wendland

In the following viewpoint, Joel Wendland criticizes the federal government's policies on AIDS. He argues that these policies have benefited big pharmaceutical companies, which can continue to charge exorbitant prices for AIDS drugs. He concludes that these policies have resulted in the deaths of millions of people worldwide who cannot afford the drugs. Wendland is a journalist who writes on political issues and managing editor of Political Affairs *magazine.*

As you read, consider the following questions:

1. In the author's opinion, why is the federal government's approach to the global AIDS crisis harmful?
2. What does Wendland mean by the "global gag rule?"

Joel Wendland, "Against the Whole World: Bush's AIDS Policy," *Online Journal*, July 20, 2004. Copyright 2004 Online Journal. Reproduced by permission of the author.

3. According to the author, how does Bush's agenda on global AIDS help big pharmaceutical companies?

Bush's AIDS policy is a killer. AIDS took the lives of 3 million people since January of 2003, the majority of whom were in Africa. Nearly half were women. Yet Bush's spending priorities to fight HIV infections and AIDS have allocated only $350 million of the highly publicized $15 billion he promised in his 2003 State of the Union speech. More interested in pushing a far-right agenda than in saving lives, Bush is presiding over one of the worst atrocities in human history. An assessment of the Bush administration's AIDS policy shows that a far-right fundamentalist religious outlook subverts medical science for a racist, anti-gay, anti-woman agenda. Recently the administration has interwoven this dangerous worldview with the profit motive of large multinational pharmaceutical corporations. Finally, the administration has molded its general "aid as imperialism" tactics to its AIDS policy. In other words, Bush uses anti-AIDS assistance to achieve certain foreign policy goals. As a result, this cynical president has overseen the deaths of millions and tens of millions more new infections.

Ideology Subverts Science

From its first day in office, an anti-condom policy has dominated many of the social policies of the Bush administration. In his 2000 campaign, Bush ran on an outspoken anti-choice, anti-gay platform in which he declared that he had little in common politically with gays and lesbians and therefore they wouldn't find a place in his administration. This thinking flowed from his Christian right-wing fundamentalism and was common to many of his religious backers in the Christian Coalition and other far-right think tanks like the American Family Association. Many of these groups blame lesbians and gays for the social ills of the country. So it wasn't a shock when Bush adopted the "global gag rule" on his first day in office.

The global gag rule, originally instituted by [President Ronald] Reagan and removed by [President Bill] Clinton, is a funding condition that requires international programs that receive money from the US Agency for International Development (USAID) not to provide abortion-related services. This includes providing education about safe sex or contraception. The International Planned Parenthood Federation called it a signal of "the Bush administration's war against women and his overall contempt for their fundamental civil and human rights."

While the "global gag rule" is rightly seen as an attack on women's reproductive rights, it also has dramatically affected social service organizations that educate local communities on preventing sexually transmitted diseases [STDs], including HIV/AIDS. The administration used the rule to withdraw USAID funding from groups that provided abortion counseling, but it also used the rule to badger organizations that provided sex education into adding abstinence components to their programs. From the start, the administration, following a religious ideology that opposes reproductive choice and contraception instead of sound medicine, worked to supplant the accepted practice of promoting consistent condom use as the best defense against HIV and other STDs with faulty and dangerous abstinence indoctrination.

The religiously motivated abstinence doctrine has been universally condemned. Erica Smiley of Choice USA, a reproductive rights advocacy group for young women, described it as "a huge disregard for democracy in other nations" because it imposes Bush's religious views on people elsewhere. She also pointed out that it dramatically affects the ability to prevent HIV/AIDS as it froze millions in USAID funding that went directly into the distribution of condoms in countries hit hardest by HIV infections. Paul Nielson of the

UN Commission for Development and Humanitarian Aid also blasted Bush's abstinence policy as dangerous to women's lives and as likely to result in "weaken[ing] the battle against AIDS." Dr. Peter Piot of UN AIDS asserted further that "We are not in the business of morality."

Right-wing Christian morality is the motor of the administration's policy. Bush didn't limit his agenda to the abstinence doctrine, however. In May of 2002 the administration, while attending the UN Children's Summit, opposed the inclusion of language recommending condom use for the prevention of HIV/AIDS and demanded that this international summit promote abstinence programs. That summer Bush withdrew $34 million from the UN Population Fund asserting a similar argument as the "global gag order." As a result several AIDS prevention programs in African countries were forced to close. Weeks later, Bush withheld $200 million earmarked by Congress for programs in Afghanistan that included sex education and condom distribution as part of HIV/AIDS prevention.

Abstinence Ideology

At the UN Asian and Pacific Regional Population conference in December of 2003, the Bush administration exerted its abstinence ideology using its economic muscle. One participant at the conference is quoted as saying that between sessions of the conference "we witnessed the US delegation threatening at least one high-level Asian delegate with his country's loss of US foreign aid and the loss of his career" if he didn't support the US agenda. The Bush administration delegation wanted to remove a recommendation of consistent condom use as an effective measure against HIV infections in favor of promoting abstinence. . . .

The Bush administration provoked another controversy of the same brand at the 15th International Conference on AIDS in Bangkok, Thailand. First, the administration withdrew huge sums of money allocated to fund the participation of dozens of American experts at the conference in order to tighten the discipline on the pro-abstinence, anti-condom line. An international furor was sparked as a result. UN Secretary General Kofi Annan called on the world, with an implicit gesture to the Bush administration, to follow through on their pledges to fund the fight against AIDS fully. Rep. Barbara Lee (D-CA) accused the administration of undermining the fight against AIDS by pushing failed abstinence programs and drawing money away from condom distribution efforts.

Bush's prioritization of ideology over medical science has been the major influence on his choice of political appointees. Among his first appointees in 2001 was Jerry Thacker, a former employee of Bob Jones University who described AIDS as a "gay plague" and homosexuality as a "deathstyle." Bush withdrew Thacker after a heated controversy, but the anti-gay ideological component remained. In the summer of 2003, Bush appointed pharmaceutical executive and Republican Party booster Randall Tobias to head the President's Emergency Plan for AIDS (the promised $15 billion fund). While Tobias seems most concerned with pressing a corporate agenda, he has done nothing to reverse the administration's anti-science trend.

Anti-Science Ideologues

The preference for appointing anti-science ideologues sparked the Union of Concerned Scientists to circulate a petition with the support of over 4,000 scientists calling for "the restoration of scientific integrity in federal policymaking." Scientists have accused the administration of systematically, in many fields of scientific work, interfering with research and distorting science to serve its ideological ends. None of this culture of interference has had more impact than on the question of the prevention of HIV/AIDS.

Most recently Bush appointees in the Centers for Disease Control [CDC], under the direction of the Department of Health and Human Services, altered federal regulations regarding funding for HIV/AIDS prevention education programs in the US. The goal, according to [journalist] Doug Ireland, is to eliminate funding for community and school-based programs that promote condom use as the best method of HIV/AIDS prevention in favor of "failed programs that denounce condom use, while teaching abstinence as the only way to prevent the spread of AIDS." Additionally, the administration wants political appointees to screen all educational materials generated by programs that receive federal funding for 3 main things. First, they must advocate abstinence as the best method of prevention; second, they must inaccurately characterize condoms as less effective than abstinence education; and finally, they must adhere to moralistic guidelines about "obscenity" and be void of "sexual suggestiveness."

Main targets of these guidelines are programs that teach proper and consistent use of condoms. Since, in the view of the Bush administration, teaching condom use is the same as promoting sexual activity, we can expect the administration arbitrarily to force sex education programs to either emphasize abstinence and downplay or demonize condom use in order to keep funding or search for limited private sources. If Bush's preference for shifting federal resources toward private, religious charities is any sign, more and more money will continue to be shifted away from sex education and prevention programs that work to abstinence-oriented and abstinence-only programs.

Abstinence Programs Do Not Work

The main problem with abstinence programs, like other areas of Bush administration politicized science, is that they don't work. At least three major studies have shown abstinence programs—especially abstinence-only programs—fail to

Aid for HIV/AIDS Crisis in Africa

A strong majority supports US aid to address the problem of HIV/AIDS in Africa. An overwhelming majority considers the crisis quite serious and believes that it will affect Americans, though the public is divided on whether it threatens US national security. About half of the public feels the US should do more than it is to help, but strong majorities think other actors such as the Africans, pharmaceutical companies and the UN [United Nations] should do more. A majority feels the US should get involved in the problem of AIDS orphans.

Americans and the World,
"Aid for HIV/AIDS Crisis in Africa," 2005.

convince youth to avoid sex until they are married. Some 88 percent of youth who made a pledge to avoid sex until marriage as part of an abstinence program, according to a Columbia University study, broke the pledge. Sexual activity among abstinence students actually increased dramatically. Because they weren't taught condom use, youth who went through such programs were one-third more times as likely to have unprotected sex, reported a study published in the *American Journal of Sociology*. But the CDC rules elevate abstinence above the medically sound principle of condom use as the best preventative measure against HIV infection and the spread of AIDS.

Corporate Agenda Is Job One

Despite research ... by Doctors Without Borders and the University of Montpellier's Research Institute for Development in France showing generic so-called 3-in-1 anti-AIDS drugs to be as effective in fighting the disease as costlier brand name drugs, a group aligned with the Bush administration attacked makers of generic AIDS drugs at the recent international conference in Bangkok, Thailand. Agence France-Presse reported that an advisor of Bush heads this group, which took out a full-page ad in the *Bangkok Post*. The Bush-affiliated group, in an effort to influence the outcome of the conference—numerous international conferences have in recent years usually have pitted the Bush people against the world and the international scientific community—attacked Cipla, an India-based company that made the 3-in-1 drugs. Bush's people described the drug as ineffective and unsafe. What is most disturbing to the Bush administration is that Cipla and other generic producers may reduce the annual cost of anti-AIDS drugs from around $10,000 to just several hundred dollars per person.

The administration's response to its critics has been to demand that the world look at its financial "generosity" in contributing to the fight against AIDS. Indeed, in his 2003 promise to deliver $15 billion over the next five years, Bush seemed to make a break from the slow-moving, underfunded policies of previous presidents. Closer scrutiny of the reality behind the public relations promise shows a return to the dangerous Reagan days.

Only $350 million in new money of the $15 billion had been disbursed in the year and a half since the promise even though Congress made $2.4 billion available. A $500 million payment [in 2004] to the Global Fund to Fight AIDS, the acclaimed UN-related multilaterally controlled fund organized in the 1990s to deliver large scale treatment and prevention resources to hardest hit regions, . . . was "late money," according to Salih Booker of Africa Action. This money had been promised in 2003 and allocated in the 2004 budget. Bush seemed to wait for a useful photo opportunity to make a delivery of the payment, which coincidentally took place just about 15 days before the 15th International Conference on AIDS. The late delivery was an attempt to stifle criticism from the international community over controversial aspects of the Bush AIDS policy.

Shrinking Funding

Meanwhile, the amount contributed to the Global Fund to Fight AIDS will shrink by 64 percent [in 2005], prompting some anti-AIDS activists to predict the fund's impending bankruptcy. Bush's $15 billion promise, says Paul Davis of Health GAP, is far short of what is needed. "[H]is five-year plan to treat 2 million people," insists Davis, "means that 13 to 15 million people with AIDS will die during that same time period." Health GAP argues that the US needs to chip in about $30 billion over the same period to fight the disease adequately.

Delaying delivery of resources, drugs, treatments, and research has been the hallmark of the Bush policy on AIDS since 2003. First, the administration's grants made through the $15 billion fund provided no money to purchase generic drugs. When that proved to be unpopular, the administration developed a "let's research and hold conferences about generic drugs" approach; meanwhile AIDS patients died. Then, [in May 2004], the administration promised to speed up the approval of generic drugs by asking the US Food and Drug Administration (FDA) to oversee the approval process. The problem is that the World Health Organization (WHO) had already undertaken most of the work Bush planned to hand over to the FDA. This proposal to duplicate WHO's work delayed the delivery process further and paralleled the administration's unilateralist approach to most major international issues; more AIDS patients died. According to Jim Lobe, writing for *Foreign Policy in Focus*, Bush's struggle over unilateral control of the global AIDS policy costs the lives of 8,000 people a day. According to UN estimates, 25 million of the 38 million infected with HIV worldwide live in southern Africa, while 7.6 million people living in Asia are infected.

The delay of resources cost lives, but in the Bush administration's view it serves a useful corporate purpose. Jen Cohn of Health GAP was quoted as pointing out that "by creating a parallel process, they're making it much more expensive and time-consuming. . . . By forcing the generic manufacturers to go through more hoops, they're ensuring Big Pharma . . . will get market share before generics get on the scene." The Tobias appointment was crucial in the development of these tactics.

By the time the administration's delegation arrived in Bangkok [in July 2004], the delay strategy was scrapped for an all out assault on generic manufacturers. Perhaps, the administration plans simply to wield its large financial stick to force the international community to do what it wants. Or perhaps it has deployed the anti-generic movement as a means of giving its more "moderate" delay tactics and anti-science ideology time to appear as a rational alternative and gain acceptance from sections of the international community.

Corporate Profits

To the present moment, religion and corporate profits have served as the ideological and economic bases for the Bush policy on AIDS. The main barrier to maximizing the effect of the policy is the international community. To sidestep the world, Bush has adopted a program of trying to bankrupt the multilateral organizations developed over the last two decades in the UN. He is fighting to replace multilateral oversight over sex education, prevention of infection, and treatment of AIDS with his unilateralist approach akin, in his words, to the "war on terror," which *The Nation* editors recently noted as having failed so miserably. Far from an emergency plan, the Bush AIDS plan is another tool to promote a foreign policy of providing aid to his friends and forcing his enemies into greater carnage.

[In 2002,] prominent economist Jeffrey Sachs, now a special adviser to UN Secretary General Kofi Annan, called on African countries to unilaterally cancel their debt and redirect the resources used for debt servicing to fight AIDS among other pressing domestic needs. Sachs' call needs to be revisited. The call for funding generics with oversight and approval through existing UN organizations should be supported. Most of all, we need an administration that will fully fund the Global Fund and will value people's lives over corporate profits and religious ideology.

We need an administration that isn't racist and homophobic and will follow scientific guidelines for the prevention and treatment of the disease. We need an administration that will regard the AIDS pandemic as a crisis not a source of profits, which currently afflicts nearly 40 million people—4 of 5 of whom live in Asia or Africa. We need an administration that will allocate the $30 billion most anti-AIDS activists and scientists believe will be necessary to fight the disease adequately over the next 5 years. We need an administration that will fight for cheaper generic drugs that have already been proven to work against the disease and are already saving lives. We need an administration that will promote effective preventative measures like condom use. We need an administration willing to work with, not against, the international community to move the most resources to hardest hit regions and not use AIDS money as a cynical and deadly foreign policy tactic. We need to dump Bush in order to move forward against AIDS.

| "There [is] only one way to fight an epidemic, which [is] to identify the carriers."

Mandatory HIV Testing Will Save Lives

David Horowitz

In the following viewpoint, David Horowitz argues that mandatory HIV testing would be a huge help in successfully containing the AIDS epidemic. He contends that only by identifying the carriers of the virus can nations successfully fight the epidemic. Horowitz is a lifelong civil rights activist, the author of numerous political books, and president of the Center for the Study of Popular Culture, in Los Angeles.

As you read, consider the following questions:

1. According to Don Francis, as quoted by Horowitz, what is the best way to fight an epidemic like AIDS?
2. How would mandatory HIV testing impact the fight against HIV/AIDS, in the author's opinion?
3. Why is criticism of mandatory HIV testing wrong, according to Horowitz?

David Horowitz, "Silent Slaughter," FrontPageMag.com, June 10, 2003. Reproduced by permission.

Since 1981 more Americans have died from AIDS than died in the Second World War—468,000 to be exact. About 40,000 new AIDS cases are reported in the United States every year. About half of the victims are under 25 years of age.

Identifying Carriers

Back in the 1980s, when most of the dead (about 350,000 of them) were still alive, I interviewed Don Francis, an immunologist and epidemiologist for the Centers for Disease Control [CDC], who was a generally recognized hero of the battle against AIDS. Francis had been the CDC official in charge of the battle against the Hepatitis B epidemic in the 1970s. I asked him how epidemics are fought. He said that there was really only one way to fight an epidemic, which was to identify the carriers of the infection and to separate them from those in their path. How to manage this separation, he said—whether by quarantine, education or other methods— was a political question.

I then asked him whether testing was important in this process. He said it depends on whether the symptoms manifest themselves on the body's surface, particularly the face of the victim immediately, or whether they are latent and difficult to detect when the infection is present. With the HIV virus a person can be a carrier for a decade without symptoms. It seemed obvious that mandatory testing would be a hugely important factor in any effort to contain the AIDS epidemic, yet at the time there was no testing and in fact the opposition to it was fierce.

Opponents of testing, which included the entire leadership of the gay community and the Democratic Party, maintained that tests could not be kept confidential and that AIDS carriers would thus become the targets of persecution. I asked Francis if this were a reasonable fear. He said, "We have been studying gay diseases since before Stonewall [the demonstra-

Why Should AIDS Testing Be Different?

Pregnant mothers are routinely tested for tuberculosis, hepatitis B, and syphilis; testing for chlamydia and group-B streptococcus is also common under certain circumstances. Newborn babies are routinely tested, without the mothers' permission, for phenylketonuria and hypothyroidism. Patients admitted to hospitals may undergo a variety of blood tests, depending on their symptoms, the tests being performed as a matter of course, without necessarily informing the patient or asking explicit permission. . . .

HIV testing, in contrast, is almost always voluntary—which means it is done either at an anonymous-testing site or with a person's explicit permission (and which usually means also that the person being tested must sign a release). At the federal level HIV testing is required only of immigrants entering the country, foreign-service and military personnel, and federal-prison inmates. At the state level routine testing is prohibited everywhere except under narrowly defined circumstances.

Chandler Burr, Atlantic Monthly, *June 1997.*

tion that launched the gay liberation movement in 1969] and I don't know of a single case of breach of confidentiality."

I asked him when there would be mandatory testing in the United States. He answered, "When enough people are dead."

Apparently, 468,000 dead are not enough.

The Damage Has Been Done

There are still no federal laws requiring testing for the AIDS virus or reporting of AIDS infections. There is no move to close public infection sites like bathhouses and sex clubs. The state of California, which has the second most cumulative

AIDS infections in the country (124,000), publishes a "Brief Guide to California's HIV/AIDS Laws, 2002," which is posted on the Internet. The very first section of the Guide is titled, "Voluntary HIV Testing." It begins: "For most individuals outside the criminal justice system, the decision to test for HIV is a voluntary one."

The very next section is titled "Prohibitions Against Mandatory Testing," and informs citizens that the "Health and Safety Code Section 120980 prohibits HIV testing to determine suitability for employment . . . and . . . insurance." State laws also prevent doctors and medical workers who perform the voluntary tests from reporting the names of individuals to public health authorities. There is thus no contact tracing to inform sexual partners of the person infected that they may have contracted the virus as well. In other words the AIDS virus is protected by law so that it can pursue its silent course through the body of the nation affecting tens of thousands of individuals who do not know they have it (by some estimates half of those infected) and who are putting others in danger through contact.

On June 4, [2003,] the *Seattle Times* reported that new AIDS cases had nearly doubled in the last year and are expected to increase by another 60% [in 2003]. "It's the most dramatic increase since the beginning of the epidemic," the *Times* quoted Dr. Bob Wood, director of AIDS Control for the Public Health Department in Seattle's King County. "One of the most important things you can do in HIV prevention is make sure people know if they are positive or negative," Wood said. "Studies show that people make major changes in behavior when they learn their status."

Well, yes.

How Has This Happened?

How did this state of affairs come to pass? How have 463,000 young Americans been allowed to die without being protected by public health authorities? Without the government intervening to deploy the most basic measure that could save them? How have both political parties remained silent or collusive in this dereliction of duty? How can the media have ignored—as they have—a policy decision that has meant serious illness and death for so many people? How can reporters have ignored a story about the needless suffering and deaths of hundreds of thousands of people whom proven and established health methods might have saved? Why has there been no interrogation of the special interests responsible for derailing the health system, specifically AIDS groups who have benefited by receiving most of the government AIDS funds— billions upon billions of dollars, allocated to "fight" the epidemic but in fact consumed in ministering to its hapless victims?

The answer is, on the one hand, that Democrats had so surrendered to the ideology of victimization that they were unable to withstand the pressures of the AIDS activists whose self-destructive political correctness won the day. It was convenient for the Democrats not to insist on hard choices for the stricken community but instead to allow AIDS activists to blame Ronald Reagan and Republican "homophobia" for the epidemic. It was good politics to ignore the reality—the epidemic was fed by a determination to disregard public health risks once the virus was discovered and to continue sexual practices that were (and are) reckless in the circumstances.

Republicans understood the policy issue but were too cowardly to confront it. One of the sources of the cowardice is a continuing affliction of the party, which is its lack of clarity on the issue of homosexuality itself. If Republicans were clear that their task as a political party is not to manage private morality, they could have responded to the crisis of a vulnerable community whose leaders have betrayed it. Compassion for the victims of the epidemic, whose government has failed to protect them, should have inspired Republicans to support the public health measures that have been discarded. But so far it hasn't.

Republicans and Democrats alike should consider the implications of what has happened. The very activists who assaulted and undermined the public health system are currently mounting new assaults on traditional institutions that are vital to the health of America's communities. Holding them to account for the damage they have already done would be a first step in stopping them from doing more.

> "Whether it's the 'war on drugs' or the 'war on terrorism,' Americans have become conditioned now to the loss of privacy. President Bush has also declared a 'war on AIDS.'"

Mandatory HIV Testing Violates Privacy Rights

Robert DeKoven

In the following viewpoint, Robert DeKoven considers a Wisconsin law that allows schools to test students for HIV. He posits that the Wisconsin law will provide the legal basis for conservatives to pass a more encompassing law, which he feels is a violation of the right to privacy and will stigmatize those who are infected with HIV. DeKoven is a professor at California Western School of Law in San Diego.

As you read, consider the following questions:

1. According to DeKoven, what are the origins of the Wisconsin law that allows schools to test students for HIV?

Robert DeKoven, "Mandatory HIV Testing—Does Anyone Remember Ryan White?" *Gay and Lesbian Times*, April 19, 2004. Copyright 2003 Uptown Publications. Reproduced by permission.

2. On what grounds does the author object to the Wisconsin law?

3. How does DeKoven define the right to privacy, and how does it clash with mandatory HIV testing?

A [2004] Wisconsin law that allows teachers to have students tested for HIV could lead to mandatory HIV testing for students in the schools. The new law merely adds school officials to the list of others—paramedics, police—that may order an HIV test for an individual who may have contaminated them with blood.

The story behind the bill involves a teacher, Cheryl Hartman, who teaches emotionally disturbed adolescents. She says these students can become violent. When restrained, they may bite. Biting, of course, has a low probability of transmission of HIV. But [in 2001] a student went into a violent rage, broke a window, sliced his arm, and some of his blood spattered in Hartman's eye. She washed her eye out immediately, fearing that she might have contracted HIV, though there was no proof that the student was HIV positive. She may have *thought he was gay* because she said that "these students" are sexually active and may also be drug-users. Yet she had no reason to believe this student was HIV positive.

Nevertheless, she wanted the student tested for HIV, but his parents refused. Hartman had to go to court and get a court order to have him tested. While a burden, this is still the best approach. School officials will want to test students to avoid liability, workers' comp and disability issues with teachers.

But under the new law, school officials—including teachers and janitors—could order students tested for HIV. Teachers, however, would need to show a doctor that a student exposed them to blood. The teacher would also have to take an HIV test within a specified time period. Teachers' unions supported the bill, but made clear that they don't support mandatory testing for students and teachers.

Confidential or Anonymous Testing

Anonymous test sites are highly recommended because:

- The quality of the education and counseling that is provided is very good.
- The testing is usually free.
- The testing is reliable and automatically includes confirming tests.
- It protects you from risks of discrimination or adverse impact, especially in applications for insurance.
- Sometimes even taking an HIV test, regardless of the result, might cause an insurance application to be refused.

"Comprehensive Guide to HIV Testing," 2005. www.aids.org.

Concerns About the Law

The new law concerns me because kids skin their knees on playgrounds, or get cuts in sports. If teachers can order a test if the teacher has been exposed, it's possible for teachers to order such tests on behalf of other students. Being HIV positive or *perceived to be positive* still bears a harsh social stigma.

Some may remember Ryan White and his family. Upon learning White was positive, some people in Kokomo, Ind., tried to kick him out of school. They burned down his family home. The right[-wing conservatives] tried to keep HIV-positive students out of school.

The national hysteria has subsided, and in the ensuing 20 years there have been no reported HIV cases resulting from transmission from student-to-student, student-to-teacher, or teacher-to-student. So this new law is unnecessary and marks yet another effort by the right to limit privacy rights. The fact that students perceived to be gay could become the targets of this law remains inescapable. That's why a federal court should strike down this law on privacy grounds and keep testing of students in the hands of judges.

There's nothing illegal about being HIV positive. No court has approved of schools conducting HIV tests or pregnancy tests under any circumstances. The right wing would like nothing more than to have mandatory STD [sexually transmitted disease], HIV, and pregnancy testing in the schools. Just as "drug tests" act as a deterrent to drug use, they argue, so, too, would mandatory STD tests. The test results would be reported to parents, and parents would learn that their kids are sexually active.

Loss of Privacy

Whether it's the "war on drugs" or the "war on terrorism," Americans have become conditioned now to the loss of privacy. President Bush has also declared a "war on AIDS". So get ready: As HIV testing has become very simple (a swab in the mouth, and results in 20 minutes), we can certainly expect to see HIV testing become far more pervasive. But before mandatory HIV testing becomes politically tenable, look for conservatives to use the Wisconsin law as basis for a federal law, requiring states receiving federal funds for education (which is all 50) to allow school officials to test for HIV. My suspicion is that it will be a matter of time before Congress requires mandatory STD testing for high school and college students.

Here's why: The *Journal of School Health* reported that one-half of new HIV infections are occurring in people under age 25. Even more startling is the statistic that 50 percent of college students will contract an STD. While mandatory and random (where there's no suspicion) tests have only been approved for the presence of alcohol or drugs, the Supreme

Court could find that the government has an interest in preventing disease transmission and [that] this outweighs privacy concerns.

> "Even if the US provided the full
> amount Congress authorized, the
> contribution still falls short of a US
> fair-share contribution to an adequate
> global response."

The United States Should Do More to Fight the Global AIDS Crisis

Global AIDS Alliance

According to the Global AIDS Alliance in the following viewpoint, the federal government has failed to live up to its promises to address the global AIDS crisis. The alliance advocates a multilateral approach, which means partnerships with other countries, international organizations, and charities. Founded in 2001, the Global AIDS Alliance is a nonprofit organization working to address the global AIDS crisis.

As you read, consider the following questions:

1. How many people does the CIA estimate will be infected with HIV by 2010, according to the alliance?

Global AIDS Alliance, "President Bush's Performance to Date on the Global AIDS Crisis," http://www.globalaidsalliance.org/policyupdate.com, December 2003. Reproduced by permission of the Global Aids Alliance.

2. According to the authors, how has President George W. Bush failed to fulfill his promises on AIDS?

3. How have international religious and aid organizations reacted to Bush's actions, according to the authors?

More than 3 million people died [in 2003] from AIDS. More than 20 million people have already died from AIDS and at least 40 million are infected. By the end of the decade, the CIA predicts that as many as 100 million people will be infected around the world. The latest data show that the epidemic is now rapidly spreading across Asia and the Americas as well as in Africa.

President George W. Bush made a stirring commitment to emergency action on the global AIDS epidemic in his State of the Union Address in January 2003. His advisors know the issue is central to the effort to project a strong global compassion agenda. . . .

The UN says the single biggest obstacle to really tackling AIDS remains lack of funding for effective programs for prevention, treatment and care. So, the question that should be asked is, "How well is President Bush living up to his promise of emergency action on AIDS?" And, "How well does his effort contribute to what the World Health Organization now says is required to expand treatment on a global basis?"

Bold No More

Sadly, the President seems to have forgotten his bold call to action:

- The White House's Director of National AIDS Policy has written to Congress at least three times since the President's Africa trip to try to stop Congress from providing full funding to critically-needed global AIDS programs. The President has used distortions and half-truths about Africa to block expanded funding that would benefit all developing countries fighting AIDS.

This effort has been partially successful in slowing the response to AIDS, and the result is that spending in 2004 will be much less than what was promised in the AIDS bill the President signed [in 2003]. . . .

- Under the President's spending plan, the US will provide just 16% of what the UN has stated is needed for a minimal response to AIDS . . . ($10.5 billion), in contrast to the 33% the US has provided to effective international efforts against polio and smallpox. (Equally troubling is that, with the exponential growth of the epidemic, even if the US provided the full amount Congress authorized, the contribution still falls short of a US fair-share contribution to an adequate global response.)

- While publicly proclaiming his support for the Global Fund to Fight AIDS, Tb [tuberculosis] and Malaria, behind the scenes the Fund's chairman, Secretary [of Health and Human Services] Tommy Thompson, is working to undermine the multilateral initiative. Because of White House pressure, the Global Fund will likely cut its grant-making in half. Europe has now far outpaced the US in donations to this innovative and cost-effective funding mechanism.

- AIDS is growing fastest in the world's most populous regions, but these areas are virtually ignored by the President's approach. AIDS and Tb in these regions have been identified as threats to global security by the US government's National Intelligence Council. Regional nuclear powers (China and India) are at risk for societal disruption.

- The President's Global AIDS Coordinator, Randy To-bias, is devising the implementation of the Bush plan largely without the involvement of people living with AIDS or other affected communities. Important questions about the implementation of abstinence-until-marriage programs and support for groups that disparage condoms remain unaddressed.

• While the much-celebrated AIDS legislation passed in May [2003] directed the White House to pursue deeper debt relief for countries fighting AIDS, President Bush has made no progress on the issue, flagrantly disregarding the will of Congress.

• While stating his initiative on AIDS would use the cheapest available medications, the President is negotiating a Central America Free Trade Agreement and a wider Free Trade Agreement of the Americas that will undermine the price competition required to ensure broad access to medications for AIDS and other illnesses. The Bush approach threatens one of the world's most successful anti-AIDS programs, that of the Brazilian government.

• The President is also failing to take sufficient action to address the AIDS epidemic in the United States. Instead of ramping up action as the epidemic grows, the Bush Administration has recommended flat funding or actual decreases in the federal AIDS safety net. . . . The number of people on waiting lists to receive assistance in accessing AIDS medication continues to grow.

A Funding Shortfall

The White House effort to stop Congress from fully funding AIDS programs at the [promised] $3 billion level . . . has provoked strong public reaction. The United States Catholic Conference, the heads of 13 Protestant and Orthodox Christian denominations, major Jewish groups, World Vision, CARE, and Save the Children have explicitly appealed to the President to back the $3 billion and even taken out newspaper ads calling for action. The Congressional Black Caucus, the NAACP [National Association for the Advancement of Colored

No Funds in the Bank

The bill we passed [in May 2003], an authorization bill, authorized $15 billion over 5 years to combat AIDS, tuberculosis and malaria. It is an important step forward. It showed that we are beginning to take the AIDS pandemic seriously. But before we all applaud ourselves and pat ourselves on the back, let's have a dose of reality. This was an authorization bill. It does not appropriate any money.

For all intents and purposes, it is like writing a check without enough money in the bank. I can recall a meeting on a different subject where someone was offering a pledge of close to $1 billion to fund an initiative. Kidding around, I said: I will double that. I will give you my check for $2 billion. In fact, I had $138 in a checking account.

That is what we have done here. By passing the AIDS authorization bill, we have promised to write a check without enough money in the bank.

Patrick Leahy, "Statement: President Bush's Budget Slashes Global Health Efforts," May 23, 2003.

People], [U-2's] Bono and others have issued appeals. 52 African heads of state signed a declaration calling for the $3 billion, and Africa's foremost church leader, Archbishop Ndungane of South Africa, has publicly rebuked the President for failing to back full funding. Dozens of editorials in major US newspapers have called on Bush to reverse course and back full, immediate funding.

The public outcry over Bush's go-slow approach has led to a startling development on Capitol Hill. 89 Senators, including previous backers of the Bush position, voted for an 18% increase ($289 million) in AIDS funding, significantly above the President's request. The startling defiance of the President by Senate Republicans, led by Senator DeWine (R-OH), dramatically showed how out of touch the President has become on the funding issue. . . .

Sadly, the President has chosen to put the vast majority of the new funding for AIDS programs into programs the US controls and operates, rather than the effective Global Fund. AIDS advocates are hopeful that the President begins backing a fully multilateral response to AIDS, the kind that polls show Americans are ready to support, rather the current US-goes-it-alone strategy.

| *"Empowering women is key to*
| *challenging the [AIDS] pandemic."*

Empowering Women in Developing Nations Is Necessary to Fight AIDS

Jennifer Davis

Jennifer Davis argues in the following viewpoint that African women are particularly at risk of HIV/AIDS because of poverty and gender inequalities. Only through empowering women can the problem of AIDS in Africa be addressed, she contends. Davis is a member of the board of the Washington Office on Africa, an ecumenical advocacy organization founded in 1972 that advocates for a fair American policy toward Africa.

As you read, consider the following questions:

1. Which country in Africa has had some success in fighting AIDS, according to Davis?

2. In Davis's view, why are African women so vulnerable to the spread of AIDS?

3. According to the author, how can empowering women

Jennifer Davis, "Gender and AIDS in Africa," http://www.woaafrica.org/aids20.htm, February 9, 2004. Reproduced by permission of the Washington Office on Africa.

help in the fight against AIDS?

In 1997, worldwide, 41% of all HIV-positive adults were women. Four years later over 47% of the total 37.2 million adults infected were women.

Sub-Saharan Africa is the region most disastrously affected by the HIV/AIDS epidemic. Some 3.4 million new infections in 2001 brought the number of African women, men and children living with the disease to 28.1 million.

There are now more women than men living with the virus in Sub-Saharan Africa, where fifty-five percent of all HIV-positive adults are women.

Some African countries are fighting back. UNAIDS [the United Nations AIDS office] reports that in Uganda, the first African country to have subdued a major HIV/AIDS epidemic, prevalence in pregnant women in urban areas has fallen for eight years in a row, from a high of 29.5% in 1992 to 11.25% in 2000.

HIV, Poverty, and Inequality

Twenty years ago, early in the HIV/AIDS epidemic, women rarely figured among the infected. But as the pandemic explodes, it is increasingly clear that women are being infected and are dying because they are women. In June 2001, Mozambique's Prime Minister, Dr. Pascoal Mocumbi, urging his fellow political leaders at the UN General Assembly Special Session on AIDS (UNGASS) to stop avoiding critical issues, underscored the need to recognize that the primary means by which AIDS is spread in Sub-Saharan Africa is risky hetero-sexual sex. This goes beyond a health issue, he indicated, for "unlike the communicable killer diseases we have encountered most often in the past, HIV/AIDS is transmitted through the most intimate and private human relationships, through sexual violence and commercial sex; *it proliferates because of women's poverty and inequality.*"

In Mozambique, he reported, the overall rate of infection among girls and young women is twice that of boys their age:

> Not because the girls are promiscuous, but because nearly three out of five are married by age 18, 40% of them to much older, sexually experienced men, who may expose their wives to HIV/AIDS. Abstinence is not an option for these child brides. Those who try to negotiate condom use commonly face violence or rejection.

Power and Prevention

Continuing gender discrimination creates life-threatening dangers for Africa's women. "There has rarely been a disease so rooted in the inequality between the sexes," Stephen Lewis, UN Secretary-General [Kofi] Annan's Special Envoy for HIV/AIDS in Africa, told a reporter at the end of 2001. The entire continent needs to understand that "women are truly the most vulnerable in this pandemic, that until there is a much greater degree of gender equality women will always constitute the greatest number of new infections." He underscored "the degree of cultural oppression that has to be overcome before we really manage to deal with the pandemic" as he outlined the situation of millions of women who are effectively sexually subjugated and forced into sex which is risky without condoms, "without the capacity to say no, without the right to negotiate sexual relationships."

Women at Risk

Biology works against women, as the virus spreads more rapidly from male to female than from female to male. For physiological reasons, women who have intercourse with men are more vulnerable to HIV infection than their partners. The virus has an easier time surviving in the vagina than on the surface of the penis; vaginal scrapes and cuts which occur during violent or coerced sex increase infection risks and semen carries a heavier viral load than the fluids of the vagina.

Women Are Vulnerable

Evidence ... suggests that a large share of new HIV infections are due to gender-based violence in homes, schools, the workplace and other social arenas. Forced or coerced sex renders a woman even more vulnerable to infection, and the younger she is, the more likely it is that she will contract HIV.

Women and girls are physiologically more vulnerable to infection, and gender-based inequities compound their risks. They are more likely to be poor and powerless, have less education, less access to land, credit or cash, and to social services.

Grinding poverty, along with a lack of education and productive resources, multiplies the chances that girls and women will sell sex as their only economic option. In AIDS-affected communities, 'survival sex' has become common currency—traded for food, cash, and 'shelter'—even for education.

Conflicts—and the attendant violence and poverty— exacerbate these human rights abuses as communities disintegrate and basic services are destroyed. Rape is a well-known instrument of war. And women and children are often exposed to sexual violence in crowded, unsafe camps for refugees or the displaced.

"How Does HIV/AIDS Affect Girls and Women?"
UNICEF Fact Sheet, *2005. www.unicef.org.*

HIV is also a gender issue, and whereas sex is biological (and fairly immutable), gender is socially defined. Gender is what it means to be male or female in any particular society. Gender shapes the opportunities one is offered in life, the roles one might play, the kind of relationships one might have. While, historically different cultures construct gender in various ways, there are consistent differences between women's and men's roles, access to productive resources and to decision making. Whatever the superstructure, the reality around us is that the foundations always incorporate *an unequal power balance in gender relations that favors men.*

Gender inequality is fueling the HIV/AIDS epidemic because it deprives women of the ability to say no to risky practices, leads to coerced sex and sexual violence, keeps women uninformed about prevention, puts them last in line for care and life-saving treatment and imposes an overwhelming burden on them to care for the sick and dying.

Saying no is not an option in many societies, where a culture of silence surrounds sex and dictates that "good" women are expected to be ignorant about sex and passive in sexual interactions. This makes it difficult for women to be informed about risk reduction, and even more difficult, even if they are informed, for women to pro-actively negotiate safer sex or the use of condoms. A study in Zambia revealed that only 11% of the women interviewed believed that a married woman could ask her husband to use a condom even if she knew him to have been unfaithful and infected.

The widespread traditional expectation of virginity for unmarried girls increases young women's risks of infection because it restricts their ability to ask for information about sex, out of fear that they will be branded as sexually active. In 17 African countries surveys indicated that over half of the girls did not know any way of protecting themselves from HIV. HIV infection rates among young African women aged 15–19 in some regions are five to six times higher than for young men.

The strong norms of virginity and the culture of silence that surrounds sex make seeking information and accessing treatment for sexually transmitted diseases highly stigmatizing both for adolescent and adult women. Women can face a tragic set of circumstances when the male head of their household dies—the husband's family often blames the widow and may refuse to accept her or her children into the family support system. The law rarely allows the woman to inherit her husband's land and property. That stigma, coupled with fear, has even produced lynch mobs in communities, when women are discovered to have the disease, or—as in the case of young South African activist Gugu Dhlamini—courageously reveal their HIV status.

Women's economic dependency increases their vulnerability to HIV. Although women are the primary producers of food across much of Africa they rarely own the land, have rights of inheritance or earn an income from their labor. Their poverty and this economic dependence often make it impossible for women to negotiate the terms of their relationships or remove themselves from relationships that put them at risk. It may force them to endure high levels of domestic violence, which both increases their chance of contracting HIV/AIDS and deters them from seeking testing and treatment. With few opportunities to earn livelihoods independent of men, women may turn to exchanging sex for favors or are even forced into commercial sex, an occupation which places them at enormous risk.

Women's access to and use of services and treatments is also affected by the power imbalance that defines gender relations. A 1999 Tanzanian study showed that while men made the decision to seek voluntary counseling and testing independent of others, women felt compelled to discuss testing with their partners before accessing the service. Initial Africa-based surveys are revealing that when anti-retroviral therapies become available, men receive a larger percentage of the treatment due to discriminatory distribution by health facilities. Women are the first to take care of their sick partners, children and families and to comfort the dying. They are the last to get life-saving treatment.

Women often only discover that they are HIV infected when they are pregnant and visit pre-natal clinics. The risk of mother-to-child transmission is high, but women are often offered little to help them reduce the risks, which might include anti-retroviral therapy, the more recently developed drug *nevirapine*, advice to make informed decisions about the alternative dangers of breastfeeding and of breast-milk substitutes and ongoing care, and counselling and support. Where treatment has been offered it has involved only a brief period, to prevent infant infection, leaving the mother to face the cruel prospect of her own death and the abandonment of her orphaned children.

Conflict situations, where rape is used as a weapon of war, are another horrific source of the spread of the pandemic, as the virus is spread through sexual violence. In Rwanda today, women who were raped in the genocide are now dying of AIDS, so for them the genocide continues.

Empowering Women

Leadership failures, cowardice, denial and avoidance have all contributed to the exploding pandemic. Lewis, Annan's Africa HIV/AIDS envoy, says: "For 20 years African leadership was largely silent, in denial . . . traumatized, paralyzed. . . . The Western world, which had the resources and knew how to deal with the pandemic . . . contributed a negligible quantity of money to Africa. In the process 17 million lives were lost and 25 million people were already infected. It is one of the most astonishing moral lapses in post-war history."

Taking Action, Providing Resources Lewis makes a powerful argument against helplessness and hopelessness: "We know how to turn the disease around, and we have the capacity at this moment to prolong and improve the lives of millions and to prevent the infection from spreading to other millions, and at the heart of it is largely the question of resources, which still isn't resolved. It can be done . . . it is just a matter of fashioning the will and the commitment to do it."

In December 2001 a WHO [World Health Organization] Commission on Macroeconomics and Health; Investing in Health for Economic Development, chaired by Harvard Professor Jeffrey D. Sachs, reported that massive investment in global health will save 8 million lives a year and generate at least $360 billion annually within 15 years. The report argues that there are very powerful links between health, poverty reduction and economic growth.

A few months earlier Secretary General Annan called for the establishment of a Global Fund on AIDS and health, a call which was endorsed by UNGASS. Noting that AIDS-specific spending from private, national and international sources currently totals $1.5–$2 billion annually in low and middle income countries, experts estimate that a global campaign against the epidemic needs $7–$10 billion annually for an effective response in those countries.

Taking Action, Empowering Women Policies that aim to decrease the gender gap in education, improve women's access to economic resources, increase women's political participation, protect women from violence and enable them to achieve their rights to sexual and reproductive health and self-determination are key to empowering women. And empowering women is key to challenging the pandemic. Women have developed a serious set of blueprints for addressing inequality—now governments need to implement the recommendations laid out in such key documents as the Convention on the Elimination of All Forms of Discrimination Against Women (CEDAW) and the Beijing Platform for Action. These need to become the guiding frameworks in the development of all HIV/AIDS prevention, treatment and care strategies.

"While microbicides are not a salvation,
they come as close to salvation as
anything else."

Microbicides Must Be Made Available to Women in Developing Nations

Stephen Lewis

In the following viewpoint, taken from his speech at the Microbicides 2004 conference in London, Stephen Lewis champions the discovery, manufacture, and widespread distribution of microbicides, a range of products such as gels, creams, or suppositories that prevent the sexual transmission of HIV/AIDS. He claims that these products are the best hope for African women at risk of HIV and AIDS. Lewis is the United Nations Secretary-General's Special Envoy for HIV/AIDS in Africa. He served as deputy executive director of the United Nations Children's Fund (UNICEF) from 1995 to 1999.

As you read, consider the following questions:

Stephen Lewis, "Women, HIV/AIDS, and Microbicides," stephenlewisfoundation.org, March 30, 2004. Reproduced by permission.

1. How do microbicides affect the spread of AIDS, according to Lewis?

2. According to the author, how does the issue of gender inequality impact African women, particularly when it comes to AIDS?

3. Why does Lewis feel that microbicides are the best solution for African women in the fight against AIDS?

There is, I will admit, a touch of amiable irrationality in racing across the ocean for a half hour speech. I want to assure you that I don't do it as a matter of course. But in this instance, it seemed to me that your kind invitation to address the Conference could not possibly be forfeited. I'm here because I think the work in which you're collectively engaged—the discovery and availability of microbicides—is one of the great causes of this era, and I want to be a part of it. It is in this room that morality and science will join together.

The Vulnerability of Women

I've been in the Envoy job for nearly three years. If there is one constant throughout that time, a large part of which has been spent traversing the African continent, it is the thus-far irreversible vulnerability of women. It goes without saying that the virus has targeted women with a raging and twisted Darwinian ferocity. It goes equally without saying that gender inequality is what sustains and nurtures the virus, ultimately causing women to be infected in ever greater disproportionate numbers.

And the numbers tell a story. It was the report issued by UNAIDS on the eve of the International AIDS Conference in Barcelona in 2002 that identified the startling percentages of infected women. And it was during a panel, at the same conference, when Carol Bellamy of UNICEF used a phrase—for the first time in my hearing—that was to become a repetitive mantra: "AIDS has a woman's face".

But the problem is that the phenomenon of women's acute vulnerability did not happen overnight. It grew relentlessly over the twenty years of the pandemic. What should shock us all, what should stop us in our tracks, is how long it took to focus the world on what was happening. Why wasn't the trend identified so much earlier? Why, when it emerged in cold statistical print did not the emergency alarm bells ring out in the narrative text which accompanied the numbers? Why has it taken to 2004—more than twenty years down the epidemiological road—to put in place a Global Coalition on Women and AIDS? Why was it only in 2003 that a UN Task Force on the plight of women in Southern Africa was appointed to do substantive work? Why have we allowed a continuing pattern of sexual carnage among young women so grave as to lose an entire generation of women and girls?

Ponder this set of figures if you will: in 2003, Botswana did a new sentinel site study to establish HIV prevalence, male and female, amongst all age groups. In urban areas, for young women and girls, ages 15 to 19, the prevalence rate was 15.4%. For young men and boys of the same age, it was 1.2%. For young women between 20 and 24, the rate was 29.7%. For young men of that age it was 8.4%. For young women between the ages of 25 and 29, the rate was 54.1% (it boggles the mind); for young men of the same age, it was 29.7%.

The Fundamental Question

Have I not addressed the fundamental question? The reason we have observed—and still observe without taking decisive action—this wanton attack on women is because it's women. You know it and I know it. The African countries themselves, the major external powers, the influential bilateral donors, even my beloved United Nations—no one shouted from the rhetorical rooftops, no one called an international conference and said what in God's name is going on? even though it felt in the 1990s that all we ever had time for were international

Would a Microbicide Eliminate the Need for Condoms?

For people who cannot or will not use condoms, and particularly for women whose partners refuse condoms, using microbicides can save lives and have a substantial impact on the HIV epidemic. In fact, researchers developed a mathematical model that shows that if even a small proportion of women in lower income countries used a 60% efficacious microbicide in half the sexual encounters where condoms are not used, *2.5 million HIV infections could be averted over 3 years.*

"About Microbicides," Global Campaign for Microbicides, *2002. www.global-campaign.org.*

conferences. It amounts to the ultimate vindication of the feminist analysis. When the rights of women are involved, the world goes into reverse.

For more than twenty years, the numbers of infected women grew exponentially, so that now virtually half the infections in the world are amongst women, and in Africa it stands at 58%, rising to 67% between the ages of 15 and 24. This is a cataclysm, plain and simple. We are depopulating parts of the continent of its women. . . .

And that's what I want to drive home. We deplore the patterns of sexual violence against women, violence which transmits the virus, but all you have to do is read the remarkable monographs by Human Rights Watch to know that for all the earnest blather, the same malevolent patterns continue. We lament the use of rape as an instrument of war, passing the virus, one hideous assault upon another, but in Eastern Congo and Western Sudan, possibly the worst episodes of sexual cruelty and mutilation are taking place on a daily basis as anywhere in the world, and the world is raising barely a finger. We have the women victims of Rwanda, now suffering full-blown AIDS, to show the ending of that story. We talk ad nauseam of amending property rights and introducing laws on inheritance rights, but I've yet to see marked progress. We speak of empowering women, and paying women for unacknowledged and uncompensated work, and ushering in a cornucopia of income-generating activities . . . and in tiny pockets it's happening, especially where an indigenous local women's leadership is strong enough to take hold . . . but for the most part, in [Winston] Churchill's phrase, it's all "Jaw, Jaw, Jaw."

The Struggle for Gender Equality

For much of my adult life, I have felt that the struggle for gender equality is the toughest struggle of all, and never have I felt it more keenly than in the battle against HIV/AIDS. The women of Africa and beyond: they run the household, they grow the food, they assume virtually the entire burden of care, they look after the orphans, they do it all with an almost unimaginable stoicism, and as recompense for a life of almost supernatural hardship and devotion, they die agonizing deaths.

Undoubtedly—and I must acknowledge this—with the sudden growing awareness internationally of what the virus hath wrought, we will all make increasing efforts to rally to the side of women. It's entirely possible that we will make more progress over the next five years than we have made in the past twenty. But I cannot emphasize strongly enough that the inertia and sexism which plague our response are incredibly, almost indelibly engrained, and in this desperate race against time we will continue to lose vast numbers of women. That is not to suggest for a moment that we shouldn't make every conceivable effort to turn the tide; it is only to acknowledge the terrible reality of what we're up against.

People say to me, Stephen, what about the men? We have to work with the men. Of course we do. But please recognize that it's going to take generations to change predatory male sexual behaviour, and the women of Africa don't have generations. They're dying today, now, day in and day out. Something dramatic has to happen which turns the talk of generations into mere moments in the passage of time.

And that, ladies and gentlemen, is where all of you come in. I'm not pretending that microbicides are a magic bullet. Microbicides aren't a vaccine. Nor do I dispute the powerful point made by Geeta Rao Gupta at the opening of the conference, that we can neither forget nor diminish the structural cultural changes so urgently required. But when so many interventions have failed, when the landscape for women is so bleak, the prospect of a microbicide in five to ten years is positively intoxicating.

The idea that women will have a way of re-asserting control over their own sexuality, the idea that they will be able to defend their bodily health, the idea that women will have a course of prevention to follow which results in saving their lives, the idea that women may have a microbicide which prevents infection but allows for conception, the idea that women can use microbicides without bowing to male dictates—indeed the idea that men will not even know the microbicide is in use? these are ideas whose time has come.

For me, while microbicides are not a salvation, they come as close to salvation as anything else I've heard about. I pray that everyone at this conference understands that the women of Africa and many other parts of the world are counting on you. It is impossible to overstate how vital is the discovery of a microbicide. If we were making progress on several other fronts, microbicides would pale. But we're not making progress, or we are making progress in such painfully minute installments, that it feels as though we're moving from paralysis to immobility. The resources of the international community should flow, torrentially, into the hands of the scientists and researchers and advocates and activists assembled here who fight the good fight, because in those hands lies life.

Periodical Bibliography

The following articles have been selected to supplement the diverse views presented in this chapter.

Africa News Service	"Africa: AIDS Progress Real but Limited," January 30, 2005.
AIDS Alert	"Global Concerns Focus on the Powerless Women Who Are Living with AIDS in the Developing World: Microbicides Might Work Where ABCs Don't," May 2004.
Lennart Bage	"HIV/AIDS in Africa: Shifting the Horizons of Development," *UN Chronicle*, September/November 2004.
Edward C. Green	"AIDS in Africa—a Betrayal," *Weekly Standard*, January 31, 2005.
Lane Jennings	"New African Visions for Combating AIDS," *Futurist*, July/August 2005.
Esther Kaplan	"The Bush AIDS Machine," *Nation*, December 20, 2004.
Alicia Keyes	"A Call to Action: Africa's AIDS Crisis Requires a Global Response," *Billboard*, December 4, 2004.
Barbara Feder Ostrov	"Slowly, AIDS Spotlight Focuses on Microbicides for Women," *San Jose (CA) Mercury News*, July 23, 2004.

For Further Discussion

Chapter 1

1. After reading the viewpoints written by Alison Motluck and the *Youth Connection*, do you think that the rate of STD infection constitutes a crisis? Why or why not? Use information from the articles to support your answer.

2. According to Christine Maggiore, many Africans diagnosed with AIDS are actually suffering from malaria, cholera, tuberculosis, or malnutrition, diseases endemic in developing countries, not HIV-related illness. How can this claim be tested?

3. Syphilis rates are increasing among gay men in the United States, according to Steve Mitchell. How should this health threat be addressed, and does the threat to public health warrant any restriction on civil rights? Explain your answer using data from the viewpoints.

4. Why do you think STDs are still spreading despite public education campaigns and availability of treatment and prevention programs?

Chapter 2

1. After reading the viewpoints by Melissa G. Pardue and Patricia Miller, discuss the benefits and/or drawbacks of abstinence-only sex education curricula, quoting from the viewpoints.

2. Joel Mowbray suggests that comprehensive sex education encourages promiscuity and the spread of STDs. Explain why you agree or disagree.

3. Considering the arguments of the authors in this chapter, what should be the government's role in funding sex education programs? What should be the government's role in designing the content of sex education programs?

4. In his viewpoint, Phill Wilson argues that the African American community should take responsibility for high-risk behaviors that increase the risk of spreading HIV, particularly among African American women. What role should religion, family, and community organizations play in controlling the spread of HIV/AIDS?

Chapter 3

1. After reading the viewpoints by Robert Rector et al. and SIECUS, do you believe taking a virginity pledge affects teen sexual behavior? Why or why not?

2. According to Angie Vineyard, "While condom use has reduced the risk for teen pregnancy and the spread of HIV, the National Institutes of Health declared that there was not enough evidence to determine that male latex condoms were effective in reducing the risk of most other sexually transmitted diseases." In your opinion, how aware of this message are teenagers, and how might this conclusion affect teen sexual behavior?

3. Katherine Ernst and Patrick Moore agree that the rate of HIV transmission in the gay community has increased in recent years, but they disagree on how to address the problem. Which author makes the most convincing argument? Why?

Chapter 4

1. After reading viewpoints by Global AIDS Alliance, Randall Tobias, and Joel Wendland, do you believe that the United States has fulfilled its funding obligations in the global fight against HIV/AIDS? Why or why not?

2. African women are particularly hard hit by the HIV/AIDS epidemic. According to Jennifer Davis, poverty and gender inequality are important factors in their vulnerability. How do think health care professionals should address the rate

of HIV/AIDS among African women, given available
resources?

3. Stephen Lewis describes the development of microbicides
as the best hope for African women in the fight against
HIV/AIDS. After reading his viewpoint, do you agree?
Why or why not?

4. Review the viewpoints by David Horowitz and Robert
DeKoven. Use evidence from their arguments to discuss
whether mandatory HIV testing in schools is a violation of
privacy. Would you object to or condone such tests in
your school or place of employment? Why or why not?

Organizations to Contact

Advocates for Youth
2000 M St. NW, Suite 750
Washington, DC   20036
(202) 419-3420 • fax: (202) 419-1448
e-mail: information@advocatesforyouth.org
Web site: www.advocatesforyouth.org

Advocates for Youth creates programs and advocates for policies that help young people make informed and responsible decisions about their reproductive and sexual health. The group also offers information, training, and strategic assistance to organizations, policy makers, youth activists, and the media in the United States and the developing world.

The Alan Guttmacher Institute (AGI)
1301 Connecticut Ave. NW, Suite 7000
Washington, DC   20036
(202) 296-4012 • fax: (202) 223-5756
e-mail: info@guttmacher.org
Web site: www.guttmacher.org

AGI is a nonprofit organization concerned with sexual and reproductive health research, policy analysis, and public education. It publishes *Perspectives on Sexual and Reproductive Health, International Family Planning Perspectives, The Guttmacher Report on Public Policy*, and special reports on topics pertaining to sexual and reproductive health and rights.

American Social Health Association (ASHA)
PO Box 13827
Research Triangle Park, NC   27709
(919) 361-8400 • fax: (919) 361-8425
Web site: www.ashastd.org

Founded in 1914 as the American Social Hygiene Association, ASHA is a nongovernmental policy organization that disseminates accurate, medically reliable information about STDs, which it provides to educators and policy makers. It also runs the Web site www.iwannaknow.org, which is directed toward teens and their questions about STDs and STD prevention.

Black AIDS Institute
1833 W. Eighth St., Suite 200
Los Angeles, CA 90057
(213) 353-3610 • fax: (213) 989-0181
Web site: www.blackaids.org

The Black AIDS Institute is an HIV/AIDS policy center that is mobilizing black institutions, organizations, and individuals to confront the epidemic in black communities. It publishes articles and commentary on the subject of HIV/AIDS in the black community as well as the 2005 report *The Time Is Now! The State of AIDS in Black America.*

Centers for Disease Control and Prevention (CDC)
National Center for HIV, STD, and TB Prevention (NCHSTP)
1108 Corporate Square
Atlanta, GA 30329
(404) 639-8040
e-mail: nchstp@cdc.gov
Web site: www.cdc.gov/

The CDC is part of the Department of Health and Human Services, which is the principal government agency in charge of providing essential health services to all Americans. The NCHSTP is responsible for public health surveillance, prevention research, and programs to prevent and control human immunodeficiency virus (HIV) infection and acquired immunodeficiency syndrome (AIDS), other sexually transmitted diseases (STDs), and tuberculosis (TB). It works with governmental and nongovernmental organizations to gather research, provide technical assistance, and evaluate programs that treat sexually transmitted diseases.

Concerned Women for America (CWA)
1015 Fifteenth St. NW, Suite 1100
Washington, DC 20005
(202) 488-7000 • fax: (202) 488-0806

Web site: www.cfa.org

CWA is a Christian women's public policy organization. The CWA has published numerous articles on abstinence-only sex education, virginity pledges, and the decline of moral values in the United States.

The Global Fund to Fight AIDS, Tuberculosis, and Malaria
Geneva Secretariat, 53, Avenue Louis-Casai, 1216 Geneva-Cointrin
  Switzerland
+41 22 791 17 00 • fax: +41 22 791 17 01
e-mail: info@theglobalfund.org
Web site: www.theglobalfund.org

Established as a partnership among governments, the private sector, and affected communities, the Global Fund aims to attract, manage, and disburse resources on AIDS, TB, and malaria all over the world to local experts in affected communities. It also monitors disease treatment and prevention programs, and publishes a number of progress reports that detail how successful these programs have been.

The Heritage Foundation
214 Massachusetts Ave. NE
Washington, DC   20002-4999
(202) 546-4400 • fax: (202) 546-8328
e-mail: info@heritage.org
Web site: www.heritage.org

The Heritage Foundation is a conservative think tank that has published numerous articles and papers on sex education, particularly the effectiveness of abstinence-only education and virginity pledges.

Manhattan Institute (MI)
52 Vanderbilt Ave.
New York, NY   10017
(212) 599-7000 • fax: (212) 599-3494

e-mail: mi@manhattan-institute.org
Web Site: www.manhattan-institute.org

MI is a public policy research organization focusing on taxes, welfare, immigration reform, education, race relations, and urban life. It publishes the *City Journal* as well as a number of articles and position papers on the topic of sex education.

Planned Parenthood Federation of America
434 W. Thirty-third St.
New York, NY   10001
(212) 541-7800 • fax: (212) 245-1845
e-mail: communications@ppfa.org
Web site: www.plannedparenthood.org

Planned Parenthood is an organization of affiliated health centers across the country that provides high-quality, afford-able reproductive health care and sexual health information to more than 5 million people every year. It also publishes *Choice! Magazine*, which promotes activism on matters of sexuality and reproductive choice.

Project Reality
1701 E. Lake Ave.
Glenview, IL   60025
(847) 729-3298 • fax: (847) 729-9744
Web site: www.projectreality.org

Project Reality is an organization that develops educational programs that teach the benefits of abstinence from sexual activity as well as from the use of alcohol, drugs, and tobacco. Curricula and promotional items are available on its Web site.

Religious Coalition for Reproductive Choice (RCRC)
1025 Vermont Ave. NW, Suite 1130
Washington, DC   20005
(202) 628-7700 • fax (202) 628-7716
e-mail: info@rcrc.org
Web site: www.rcrc.org

RCRC is a group of clergy and lay leaders from various religious organizations that was founded in 1973 to protect the reproductive rights of women. It also works to find solutions to such problems as unintended pregnancy, the spread of STDs, and the high cost of health care and health insurance. RCRC also advocates public policies that provide comprehensive sex education, affordable child care and health care, and family planning services. It publishes various denominational prayers and sermons on reproductive and sexual topics on its Web site.

Sexuality Information and Education Council of the United States (SIECUS)
1706 R St. NW
Washington, DC 20009
(202) 265-2405 • fax: (202) 462-2340
e-mail: siecus@siecus.org
Web site: www.siecus.org

Established in 1964, SIECUS is a national organization that works to promote sex education for people of all ages, to protect sexual rights, and to expand access to sexual health care. SIECUS distributes hundreds of thousands of print and electronic resources to educators, advocates, parents, researchers, physicians, and others working to expand sexual health programs and policies. It also publishes several reports on sexual health and reproductive issues, such as "The Politics of Sexuality Education" and "Getting It Together: Integrating Teen Pregnancy and STD/HIV Prevention Efforts" as well as the quarterly journal *SIECUS Report.*

True Love Waits (TLW)
One LifeWay Plaza
Nashville, TN 37234
(800) 588-9248
e-mail: truelovewaits@lifeway.com
Web site: www.lifeway.com/tlw

A part of LifeWay Student Ministries, TLW is a Christian organization for teens that promotes sexual abstinence until marriage through the sponsorship of virginity pledges. It disseminates information for young people, parents, and group leaders about the abstinent way of life.

Bibliography of Books

Consuelo M. Beck-Sague and Caridad Beck — *HIV and AIDS*. Philadelphia: Chelsea House, 2003.

Greg Behrman — *The Invisible People: How the U.S. Has Slept Through the Global AIDS Pandemic*. New York: Free Press, 2004.

Holly Cefrey — *Syphilis and Other Sexually Transmitted Diseases*. New York: Rosen, 2002.

Christine Perdan Curran — *Sexually Transmitted Diseases*. Springfield, NJ: Enslow, 1998.

Charles Ebel and Anna Wald — *Managing Herpes: How to Live and Love with a Chronic STD*. Research Triangle Park, NC: American Social Health Association, 2002.

Julie K. Endersbe — *Sexually Transmitted Diseases: How Are They Prevented?* Minnetonka, MN: LifeMatters, 2000.

Sebastian Faro — *Sexually Transmitted Diseases in Women*. Philadelphia: Lippincott, Williams & Wilkins, 2003.

Michelle M. Houle — *AIDS in the 21st Century*. Berkeley Heights, NJ: Enslow, 2003.

Susan Hunter — *Black Death: AIDS in Africa*. New York: Palgrave Macmillan, 2003.

Marjorie Little — *Sexually Transmitted Diseases*. Philadelphia: Chelsea House, 2000.

Christine Maggiore — *What If Everything You Thought You Know About AIDS Was Wrong?* Studio City, CA: American Foundation for AIDS Alternatives, 1999.

Andrew T. McPhee	*AIDS*. New York: Franklin Watts, 2000.
M. Monica Sweeney and Rita Kirwan Grisman	*Condom Sense: A Guide to Sexual Survival in the New Millennium*. New York: Lantern Books, 2005.
Katherine White	*Everything You Need to Know About AIDS and HIV*. New York: Rosen, 2001.
Diane Yancey	*STDs: What You Don't Know Can Hurt You*. Brookfield, CT: Twenty-First Century Books, 2002.

Index